Shakespeare's Dead

Shakespeare's Dead

Simon Palfrey & Emma Smith

Bodleian Library
UNIVERSITY OF OXFORD

First published in 2016 by the Bodleian Library
Broad Street, Oxford OX1 3BG
www.bodleianshop.co.uk

ISBN: 978 1 85124 247 4

Text © Simon Palfrey and Emma Smith, 2016
Images, unless specified, © Bodleian Library, University of Oxford, 2016
The transcription of MS. Ashmole 234 (Figure 21) is courtesy of the Casebooks Project team at
the University of Cambridge

Designed and typeset by Dot Little at the Bodleian Library in 11/15pt Adobe Caslon
Printed and bound by Great Wall Printing Co. Ltd, Hong Kong on 157 gsm Neo matt paper

British Library Catalogue in Publishing Data
A CIP record of this publication is available from the British Library

Contents

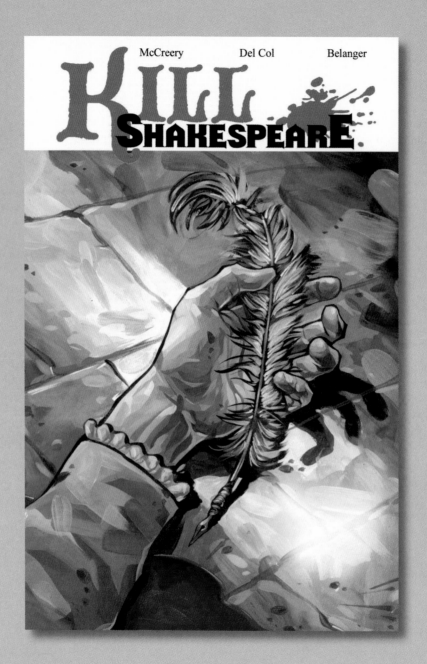

Foreword

At the 400th anniversary of his death, Shakespeare could hardly be more alive: in the theatre, in popular culture and in scholarship. The date of his death in April 1616 is commemorated in books today precisely because of the liveliness of his legacy. This dead author is immortal, preserved and renewed on the stage, on the page, and in the mind. Shakespeare's plays enact a similar paradox in their representation of his perennial dramatic theme: death. Death in Shakespeare turns out to have the contradictory quality of affirming life. In memory; in epitaph; in the living body of the actor; in the refusal to go quietly; in the return of ghosts and the missing: Shakespeare's dead turn out to be anything but. Shakespeare's works affirm life even when they are about death.

This book, and the Bodleian Libraries exhibition that it accompanies, explores this central paradox about Shakespeare's dead. We see the playful, sceptical and disruptive ways his plays and poems handle life and death. Shakespeare's sense of the afterlife is unorthodox. No-one dies of plague in his works, despite – or perhaps because - this was such a prominent threat in the London of his age. Instead, play characters die in ever more ingenious ways, from suicide to murder, and from workaday dagger to baroque pie recipe. Looking anew at the early playtexts we see how carefully death is choreographed, and how moving moments of funeral or mourning are often undercut. 'Fear no more the heat o' the sun', one of Shakespeare's most poignant elegies, is occasioned by a misapprehension. Innogen is not Fidele and nor is she dead.

'Books', wrote John Milton, 'are not absolutely dead things, but do contain a potency of life in them.' Ben Jonson described Shakespeare's collected works, published in 1623, as 'a monument without a tomb'. Thomas Bodley initially banned plays and 'baggage books' from his library, but the Bodleian's collections, from its First Folio acquired early in 1624 to Robert Burton's gift of *Venus and Adonis* and the extensive later collections of Edmond Malone, are lively monuments to Shakespeare. This book and exhibition are part of the Bodleian Libraries' contribution to the celebratory programme of events in Oxford and across the country for 'Shakespeare 2016'. Shakespeare's dead: long live Shakespeare!

Richard Ovenden
Bodley's Librarian

Figure 1 The premiss of the *Kill Shakespeare* graphic novel series is that Shakespeare's characters are on the march in defence of – or to attack – their creator. So far they have not succeeded in killing Shakespeare. Artwork by Kagan McLeod, reproduced by permission of Kill Shakespeare Entertainment.

I
Something after Death

The most famous speech in Shakespeare hinges upon the dreadful mystery of life beyond the grave:

> To die, to sleep.
> To sleep, perchance to dream. Ay, there's the rub:
> For in that sleep of death what dreams may come
> When we have shuffled off this mortal coil
> Must give us pause. …
> Who would these fardels bear,
> To grunt and sweat under a weary life,
> But that the dread of something after death,
> The undiscovered country, from whose bourn
> No traveller returns, puzzles the will,
> And makes us rather bear those ills we have
> Than fly to others we know not of?
>
> (*Hamlet*, 3.1.66–84)

Figure 3 This sixteenth-century finger-ring carries a *memento mori* in the shape of an enamelled skull. The paradox of such a richly crafted gold reminder of mortality is striking, at once an acknowledgement of worldly and of spiritual value. WA.1897.CDEF.F642 © Ashmolean Museum, University of Oxford.

Ignorance produces anxiety, bafflement and paralysis. We survive because we are afraid of what death will bring. If we knew death, implies Hamlet, no one would stay to live. Because we do not, yet because death remains, life is sustained. With deep irony, death becomes the parent of life.

The dread felt by Hamlet is not simply that we exist in the dark; nor is it that the prospect of death generates an existential terror of non-being. Curiously, it is almost the opposite of this. The fear is that we endure in death. Or, more precisely,

9

that consciousness and self-reflection endure. If death were indeed oblivion, if it brought an end to pain and frustration, to will and memory, then he would 'devoutly' wish to be dead. This is the dark longing in the speech's immortal opening line:

To be, or not to be; that is the question

Not to be is Hamlet's fondest, fiercest wish. But still *to be* when life is over would be unendurable – and so he consents to suffer.

Hamlet's perplexities touch upon the deepest spiritual questions of Shakespeare's age. It was an age of Reformation and Counter-Reformation. Shakespeare was born thirty years after Henry VIII split the English from the Roman Church, and lived his life amid the reverberating trauma. England was a Protestant state, with the monarch head of the national Church. Failure to attend Anglican services could bring strict penalties. Religious passions were inextricably linked to national security; throughout Shakespeare's life England was intermittently in conflict with the great Catholic powers, France and Spain, while Ireland, ever recalcitrant, was the constant scene of atrocity in the name of reform and the English Crown. The most ubiquitous books in the land were the newly translated Bible and John Foxe's *Book of Martyrs* (Figure 4), a huge tome canonizing the heroism of English Protestants sacrificed in the reign of 'Bloody Mary', the deluded servant of the Roman Antichrist. A copy was placed in every church in the land, linking mundane observances to the headiest of communal memories.

But private confusions, as suffered by Hamlet, may have struck even deeper. The central questions hinged upon death. Mortal life, as everyone knew, was a temporary cease before the real truth started. But what was the relation between this life and the next? How to ensure safe passage for one's immortal soul? For those brought up in the Catholic faith the answers were relatively simple. Act virtuously, observe the sacraments, confess your sins, do as the priest says, and the slate should be clean when you meet your maker. For Martin Luther, catalyst of

Figure 4 The battered condition of this 1563 edition of the book commonly known as Foxe's *Book of Martyrs* nicely echoes its contents – a series of accounts and often gruesome images of protestant suffering that gave Shakespeare's England its iconography of martyrdom. Included in the volume is the martyrdom of John Oldcastle, the model for Shakespeare's Falstaff. Bodleian Library, Douce F subt. 2, title page.

ACTES

and Monuments

of these latter and perillous dayes,
touching matters of the Church, wherein
ar comprehended and described the great persecu-
tions & horrible troubles, that haue bene wrought
and practised by the Romishe Prelates, special-
lye in this Realme of England and Scotlande, from the yeare of our Lorde a
thousande, vnto the tyme
nowe present.

Gathered and collected according to the
true copies & wrytinges certificatorie, as wel
of the parties them selues that suffered, as
also out of the Bishops Registers,
which wer the doers therof,
by Iohn Foxe.

¶ Imprinted at London by Iohn Day,
dwellyng ouer Aldersgate.

Cum priuilegio Regiæ Maiestatis. 1563

Reformation, this was a grotesque libel against God. He is perfect, all-knowing and unknowable; we are disgusting sinners, racked by appetite and terror. We know nothing and deserve less. Death is certain, damnation inevitable, life despair. There is nothing to be done about it. But then this very impotence generates the answer. We must give ourselves absolutely to God, as Christ did. Priests can no longer help as they used to. We can only be saved by the free gift of God's grace, manifested as faith in Christ's Passion, and discovered in the truth of the Gospels.

Luther discovered a perilous, radically private relationship between God and personhood, importing the priesthood of all believers. But truly to be a *believer*, with its strenuous renunciation of freedom, power and choice, is the very hardest thing. There is no end to anxiety, because there is no faith without it. The only true life is one of Christ-like torment, turning in the vortex of sin in the hope that God will bring release. Luther's doctrine of justification by faith alone had the profoundest influence upon the development of early modern self-consciousness – a consciousness defined by the immanent presence and impending horror of death.

The alarming thing about Shakespeare's age is the *presentness* of the spiritual stakes, their urgency and intimacy. When Hamlet speaks of being 'puzzled' by the enigma of death, he means more than feeling bewildered, unable to penetrate into the truth of things. It is specifically the 'will' that is frustrated – meaning volition or desire, the power to act, and to be a self-sovereign agent. Being is no more secure than knowledge – which might be radically contingent. Anything you think you know, or own – anything you think you *are* – might instantly be whipped away. And religion, with terrible justice, sets the scene. The same anxiety is found in supposed comedies:

Should I go to church
And see the holy edifice of stone
And not bethink me straight of dangerous rocks
Which, touching but my gentle vessel's side,
Would scatter all her spices on the stream,
Enrobe the roaring waters with my silks,

Figure 5 Indulgences were part of the financial and spiritual economy of Catholicism: they marked a reduction in the time the dead would spend in purgatory. Abuse of the system of indulgences was one of the focuses of Luther's attack on the church. Bodleian Library, Arch. B b.5 (1a), 1482.

Forma confessionalis·

Pateat vniuersis presentes litteras inspecturis· Qualiter deuot in xpo
diocess ad op̃s sancte cruciate p̃ Sacntissimū in xpo p̃res et dñm nrm· dñm Sixtu diuina p̃uidentia· papa quartu
ordinatum debitam fecerit ẽtributione· Quapropter auctoritate p̃efati domini nostri ipe potate hr eligendi
sibi confessorem p̃espiterum ydoneum religiosum vel seculare· qui audita diligenter eius ẽfessione absoluere cum
possit auctoritate ẽdicta ab omnib9 ẽmissis per eum excessibus et peccatis quibuslibet quantumcūq enormibus·
Etiā si talia forent ꝗpter que sedes apostolica esset ẽsulenda· Et a censuris et penis ac excõicatiõibus omnibus
A iure vel p̃ statuta quecūq ꝓmulgatis et sedi aplice reseruatis semel dūntaxat· A nõ reseruatis vero eadem sedi
totiens quotiens id petierit· Ac semel in vita et in mortis articulo plenaria omnium peccatoꝝ suoꝝ indulgentia
et remissionem impendere· Non obstãtibus quibuscūq reseruatiõibus a p̃fato pontifice· vel eius predecessoribus
sedis ꝓut in bulla data· M·CCCC· LXXXX pridie nonas decēbris pontificat9 eiusdem anno decimo plenius
continetur· In cui9 rei fidem et testimoniū Ego frater petr9 Gardian9 ꝗ predicator dueñ thona cen̄· ordinis mino-
rum subcommissarius eiusdem sanctissimi dñi nostri Sixti pape quarti super p̃efato negocio deputatus p̃esentes
litteras fieri feci· Et sigilli cruciate impressione muniri· Anno domini· M·CCCC·LXXXXij· die

Forma absolutionis·

Misereatur tui omnipotens deus ⁊c· Dominus noster Ihesus cristus per suam piissimam misericordiam te absol-
uat· Et auctoritate ei9 et beatoꝝ petri et pauli aploꝝ ac Sactissimi dñi nri pape mihi ẽmissa et tibi ẽcessa· ego
te absoluo a vinculo excommunicationis si incidisti et restituo te sacñetis ecclie ac vnioni et participacõi fideliū
Et eade auctoritate te absoluo ab omnibus et singulis criminibus delictis et peccatis tuis quãtucūq grauibus et
enormibus· Etiam si talia forent propter que sedes apostolica ẽsuleda esset ac de ipsis eadem auctoritate tibi plenariam indulgentiam et remissionem confero· In nomine patris et fily et spiritussancti Amen·

⸿ Nota ꝗ in mortis articulo adiungenda est hec clausula· Si ab ista egritudine non decesseris plenariam remissionem et indulgentiam tibi eadem auctoritate in mortis articulo conferendam reseruo·

ne a remission des pechiez. mais punist par durablemnt
les pechies veniaulx cõme les mortelz . Et pour le
souffrir et endurer. les dãm̃nez ne desiruent enuis dieu
auoir aucune rela che ne refrigere de lardeur en qy ilz sont.

And, in a word, but even now worth this,
And now worth nothing?

(The Merchant of Venice, 1.1.29–36)

Other Reformation thinkers went still further than Luther. John Calvin's doctrine of double predestination took what might seem the inevitable next step. If God is all-powerful and all-seeing, then everything that will ever be has already been determined, including each individual's personal salvation or perdition. We are pawns in a pre-written plot. The only proof of salvation is the gift of faith in Christ – but a moment's wavering, the briefest hint of doubt, might equally be proof of damnation. One's posthumous condition pre-empts the moment-by-moment emotions of life; post-mortem speculation underpins the most basic conceptions of self.

Luther resisted predestination, as he did those who denied the real presence of Christ's flesh and blood in the bread and wine of Mass. True to his Catholic upbringing, Luther saw the Eucharist as a kind of incarnation of the divine, a physical miracle of transubstantiation. Calvin, by contrast, admitted a spiritual rather than a real presence in the transaction. Other leading reformers (such as Zwingli) understood the Eucharist as a metaphor of the 'travel' between the temporal and the divine. Whatever Shakespeare's beliefs, he must have felt the pertinence of these questions to his own art. Was the Mass a highly charged piece of drama? Or was it real? How literally should we understand symbolic events? Can life spring from inanimate objects? Can life come from death? The same questions might be asked of another 'miraculous', substance-altering public event – the theatre.

As we see with these debates, religion wasn't a simple matter of Catholic versus Protestant. There were shades within shades, and deadly rivalries amid nominal allies, just as there were many affiliations between radically opposed faiths. No doubt for many people sympathies with the old faith ran deep, if not to Rome's authority then to its habits of mind, its spiritual-cum-mental geography. The

Figure 6 This illustration of hell is from the *Livre de la Vigne nostre Seigneur*, an illustrated treatise on Judgement, Hell and Heaven, depicting the scenes that fifteenth-century Europeans must have feared or hoped to encounter after death. Bodleian Library, MS. Douce 134 (fol. 90v), South East France, early 1460s.

example of the Jesuit poet and priest Robert Southwell offers striking evidence. He was a missionary for his order, secretly recruiting converts to the Catholic faith. To do so was treason. In 1592 he was imprisoned, tortured and consigned to a cavern in Newgate Prison called Limbo. After three years he was put on trial and sentenced to death. He was hanged and disembowelled, his severed head displayed as a sign of what happens to heretics. But then immediately after his execution, this pernicious traitor's poetry, written mainly to give strength to the fugitive Catholic community, was republished. It was an enormous bestseller, reaching audiences far beyond his own community and enjoying multiple reprintings over the next decades. Southwell's fate testifies to the intensity and violence of religious dissension – and yet also to the fact of profoundly shared language and emotions.

As Robert Watson observes, 'nearly all of the famous transforming achievements of the Renaissance had side effects that must have magnified the terrors of mortality'.[1] These achievements include imperial exploration, the invention of the telescope, and a renewed attention on the actual Word of scripture, studied and translated as never before. One consequence of this was the abolition of Purgatory as a popish fiction. With it went prayers for the dead. The loss was considerable. There was no longer a sanctioned way of relieving the suffering of departed loved ones. The dead were on their own, or at least severed from living human contact. Of course, to feel the loss of such comforts need not mean secretly hankering for their restitution; the convinced Protestant might at once accept and lament the fact that Purgatory didn't exist. But it was a mind-world in which these questions hung in the air; imagination would dwell upon places beyond sensory proof, perhaps even beyond possibility.

No one really knows Shakespeare's personal confessional allegiance – if indeed he had one (or many, or any). Long tradition has implicitly understood Shakespeare as a child of the Elizabethan settlement, horrified by extremes, probably loyal to Anglican orthodoxy (his children were baptised in the official church), probably mildly sceptical about clerical authority. He certainly invests little faith in priests or other would-be transcendent spiritual mediators; his most characteristic

Figure 7 This striking image of King Death parodies the iconography of royal portraiture to produce a terrifying sovereign. As the accompanying poem observes: 'all the world or is, or shall be, dead'. *The Mirrour which Flatters not*, by Jean Puget de la Serre, translated by Thomas Cary, 1658 (second edition). Bodleian Library, Vet. A3 f.1705, title page.

THE DESIGN OF THE FRONTISPICE.

LOe, *DEATH* invested in a Roab of *Ermine*,
Triumphant fits, embellished with *Vermine*,
Upon a Pile of *dead men's Skulls*, her Throne,
Pell mell subduing all, and sparing none.
A scrutinous *judgement* will the *Type* reffent,
You may imagine, 'Tis *DEATH'S Parliament.*
Upon the *World* it's pow'rful *Foot* doth tread,
For, all the world or is, or shall be dead.
One *hand* the *Scepter*, t'other holds our *Mirrour*,
In courtesie to shew poor *flesh* its *errour*:
If *men* forget themselves, *It* tells'em home,
They're *Dust* and *Ashes*, All to *this* must come.
To view their *fate* herein, some will forbear,
Who *wave* all thought of *Death* as too severe :
But know, *Death* (though it be *unknown* how *nie*)
A *Point*, on which depends *ETERNITIE,*
Either to live *Crown'd* with perpetual *Bliffe*,
Or howl *tormented* in *Hell's* dark *Abyffe.*
With *winged hafte* our brittle *lives* do pass,
As runs the gliding *Sand* i'th' *Hour-Glass.*

If more you would, continue on your *Look*
No more upon the *Title*, but the *Book.*

THE MIRROVR *which* Flatters not.

O that they were Wife, *that they* understood This,
that they would Confider *their latter* End! *Deut:* 32.29.
—— MORS fola fatetur

Quantula fint hominum corpuscula. —— *Iuvenal:*

J.P. *Sculs*

churchmen are ineffectual, belated, verbose or fraudulent; they are not hated, and not often harmful; but certainly they are not the founts of superior authority. In so far as Shakespeare invests in death-redeeming acts, the agents tend to be pagan, medicinal or *coups de théâtre*. At such moments Shakespeare's purposes are always more theatrical than confessional, often walking a tightrope between irreverence and emotion. When Shakespeare scripts a worshipful song for the dead – for Hero in *Much Ado*, or Fidele in *Cymbeline* – the character is all set to spring back to life. A revered marble icon comes to life in *The Winter's Tale* – unless it was never a statue in the first place. There are hints of Marian iconography, of death redeemed though tears and repentance – but equally of Pygmalion-style transgression, or a trick of art, or a mouldy old tale.

The American tragedian Arthur Miller wrote that 'the lasting appeal of tragedy is due to our need to face the fact of death in order to strengthen ourselves for life'.[2] But rarely does Shakespeare offer that prospect as a 'joyful hope'. Perhaps the only truly comforting vision of death in his plays is that afforded to the sick, rejected wife of King Henry in *All Is True*. It can't be a coincidence that Katherine's vision is an unapologetically Catholic one. Cast off in favour of (the Protestant) Anne Boleyn, Katherine announces herself 'sick to death' as she hears of the passing of her enemy Cardinal Wolsey. While she sleeps, an elaborate spectacle entitled 'The Vision' gives us multimedia access to her blissful reverie. The stage direction describes people in white robes and golden masks who dance around the queen and acknowledge her with a garland of bays. 'At which, as it were by inspiration, she makes in her sleep signs of rejoicing, and holdeth up her hands to heaven.' Waking from this vision, Katherine describes a 'blessèd troop' with 'bright faces' who 'promised me eternal happiness' (4.2.87–90). Her death follows swiftly. Katherine's vision of heaven brings a comfort denied to most other characters in the plays.

There are many who believe Shakespeare remained a closet Catholic (his father was at one time a recusant), disguising his true convictions in the interests of prudence and survival. It is true that many of the plays feature vestiges of Catholic rituals and assumptions and icons. Indeed the first printed text of *Hamlet* in 1603

Figure 8 An early edition of *Hamlet* (1611), one of Shakespeare's most extended engagements with mortality. Bodleian Library, Arch. G e.13.

THE
TRAGEDY
OF
HAMLET
Prince of Denmarke.
BY
WILLIAM SHAKESPEARE.

Newly imprinted and enlarged to almoſt as much
againe as it was, according to the true
and perfect Coppy.

AT LONDON,
Printed for *Iohn Smethwicke*, and are to be ſold at his ſhoppe
in Saint *Dunſtons* Church yeard in Fleetſtreet.
Vnder the Diall, 1611.

reveals a basically orthodox Catholic theology, anticipating paradisal dreams in place of the more familiar nightmares:

> For in that dream of death, when we're awaked
> And borne before an everlasting judge
> From whence no passenger ever returned –
> The undiscovered country, at whose sight
> The happy smile and the accursed damned.

(Q1)

For this Hamlet, we endure life because what is promised afterwards is our 'joyful hope'. In the more familiar text printed in 1604 and preferred ever since, we put up with it because the terrors of what comes next are unbearable. The fault lines revealed by the two *Hamlet* texts are deeply suggestive. It emerges as an uneasy palimpsest of religious doctrines, particularly where they address post-mortem existence. As Stephen Greenblatt puts it, 'A young man from Wittenberg with a distinctly Protestant temperament is haunted by a distinctly Catholic ghost.'[3] And yet, as regards Shakespeare's own beliefs about life after death, here as elsewhere the evidence is neutral, present along with much else that is contrary to it. He could inhabit any subject or spiritual position imaginable, and we might with as much justice suggest he delved in demonology.

One thing is certain: Shakespeare's work is everywhere marked by the kind of shifting, self-shadowing, forward-and-backward sensitivity that will result when foundational spiritual conditions are up for grabs. Again and again in his work we witness the separateness of the individual soul; the intermittent conviction of unworthiness; the puzzle and wonder of a world beyond knowledge; the difficulty of adequate mediation with the absolute; the fear or conviction of reprobation; the suspicion felt towards dazzling spectacle; the irony attending rituals of atonement; the struggle to take on sin, one's own or another's, as a personal burden. Perhaps above all, Shakespeare explores the possibility of self-responsibility, even in abjection and impotence. And this means the responsibility to try to construe things right, as Protestants were supposed to do with scripture: to interpret the signs, attend to the evidence, feel-out the phenomena, whatever our consciousness of blindness or stupor or anguish or unfitness.

And, of course, what holds true for Shakespeare's characters applies equally to his present readers and witnesses. As his fellow King's Men, Heminge and Condell, put it in their preface to the First Folio, 'Read him, therefore, and again, and again.' The injunction belongs to no church.

THEATRVM ANATOMICVM Lycei Patauini.

2

MEASURE FOR MEASURE

The Art of Dying

Of all Shakespeare's plays, it is the disturbing 'tragicomedy' *Measure for Measure* which is most engaged with the art of dying, and which has the most sustained imaginings of being dead. Just as contemporary anatomy theatres dissected human or animal cadavers in the full view of students and other observers (Figures 9 and 23), *Measure for Measure* conducts a forensic investigation into the causes – and the consequences – of mortality.

It is from early on a more religious play than most (it takes its title from the Gospels), with the heroine Isabella a novice in a nunnery, wishing to eschew the temptations and corruptions of the world. For Isabella questions of desire and judgement are instantly ultimate, working in a continuum that reaches from Christ and heaven to weeping angels and deserved damnation. A similar absoluteness marks government under the deputy Angelo. To break the law is to die. Hence the central plot event: Isabella's brother Claudio has had sex outside marriage (albeit to his betrothed); he has been sentenced to death; his only hope is if Isabella can persuade the strict deputy to show mercy:

> All hope is gone,
> Unless you have the grace by your fair prayer
> To soften Angelo.
>
> (*Measure for Measure*, 1.4.67–9)

Figure 9 An engraving of a contemporary anatomy theatre at the University of Padua from *Gymnasium Patavinum* by Giacomo Filippo Tomasini, 1654. The image portrays a human cadaver alone, as a scientific specimen laid out for inspection without any of the religious accompaniment – symbols of mourning, or representations of demons arresting the soul – which characterized medieval depictions of the dead. *Gymnasium Patavinum* by Giacomo Filippo Tomasini, [Udine], 1654. Bodleian Library, Douce T 265.

Notice the mixture of spiritual and profane: her fairness is her beauty, but also her honesty; her 'grace' is her feminine elegance, but also her access to divine forgiveness. Even in its simple secular action – Isabella pleading with Angelo to change his mind – the play is always implying a world beyond the grave, and trying to peep into that world's secrets:

> *Angelo*   Your brother is a forfeit of the law,
> And you but waste your words.
>   *Isabella*   Alas, alas!
> Why, all the souls that were were forfeit once,
> And He that might the vantage best have took,
> Found out the remedy.
>
>   (2.2.73–7)

Isabella takes Angelo's word, 'forfeit' – meaning that Claudio's life must be given up as the penalty for his transgression – and turns it into the universal reprobation that preceded the redeeming 'remedy' of Christ. That is, all souls were 'forfeit' – lost to perdition – before Christ's 'forfeit' brought them back to eternal life. Christ's sacrifice will not only teach Angelo the truth in renouncing worldly power, but it will substitute for Claudio's otherwise wasteful sacrifice. These substitutions get their strange compulsiveness from the seriousness, the literalness, of Isabella's Christian vision. She really *sees* these forfeited souls, turning in the vortex of damnation, just as she sees Christ, from his 'vantage' up high, taking pity.

To see what Shakespeare is up to we have to think as literally and absolutely as Isabella. It isn't just that Claudio will lose his life if Isabella fails. It is that he is *sentenced to death*. He will enter death's space, the nature of which becomes a pressing question. But the added complication is that the quality of death is not simply there, waiting to be unveiled. It hinges upon actions and minds in this world, which can materially inform the nature of our afterlife. This is why the question of preparedness for death is so important.

Figure 10 The medieval genre of the *ars moriendi* in various forms instructed the faithful how to make a good death. Bodleian Library, MS. Bodl. 423, part C (English, mid-fifteenth century), fol. 228r.

Here begynneth the boke of the crafte of dyeng

Or asmuche as the passage of deeth · of the greetnes-
nesse · of the exyle of thys worlde · for vnkonynge
of dynge · not oonly to lewde men · but also to
Religious · and deuoute psones · semeth wonderly hard and
rylous · and also right ferful · and horrible · therfore in
thys present matre · and tretys that is of the crafte of dyenge
is drawe and conteynes a short matre of exhortacyon · for
techynge & confortynge of hem that ben in poynt of deeth ·
Thys matre of exhortacyon ought sotelly to be consydred
noted · and vnderstonde in the syght of mannes soule ·
ffor douteles it is · and may be profitable generaly · to alle
trewe cristen men · to leyne · and haue craffte & knowlache
to deye wel · ¶ Thys matre & tretyse conteyneth vi ptics of cheptres ·
¶ The fyrst is of comendacyon of deeth · & konyng to dye wel ·
¶ The seconde conteyneth ye temptacyons of men yt dyen ·
¶ The thyrd conteyney ye interrogacōs yt shuld be asked of hem
that byn in her deth bed · while pey may speke & vnderstonde ·
¶ The fourthe conteyneth an informacyon with
certayn obsecracyouns to hem that shuln dye ·
¶ The fyfthe wtreyney an instruccyon to hem that shul dye ·
¶ The syxte conteyueth praiers that shulden be seyde
vpon hem yt ben a dyenge · of som men yt be aboute hem ·
The fyrst chaptre is of comendacōn of deth & of konyng to dye wel ·   Cap pm

Hough bodily deth · be moost dredful of alle
ferful thynges · as the philosophre seyth · in the
thyrd book of etykes · yet cruel deeth of ye
soule is as moche moor horrible & detestable · as the soule
is moor worthy and preyouse · than the body · as the pphete
dauid saith · Mors ptō^r pessima · The deeth of the synful
man is worst of alle dethes · But as the same pphete seyth ·
Preaosa est in conspectu dñi mors sctōr eius · The deeth of
the good men is eu preyouse · in the syght of god · what man of bodily
deeth · eu they dye · And thou shalt vnderstonde also · that
not oonly deeth of holy martyrs is so preiouse · but also the
deeth · of alle other rightful · and good cristen men · And
furthermoor the deeth douteles of alle synful men · how

Learning to die well was one of the popular self-help topics in the Elizabethan publishing industry. The medieval *ars moriendi* tradition – or the 'art of dying' – developed into a range of works on the good death (Figure 10). Urging his readers 'to die well, and to die gladly', Thomas Lupset, the humanist scholar and collaborator with Erasmus, reassured them that death was not to be feared because 'it is no new thing to die, our fathers, our grandfathers, our great foresires be gone the way that both we shall go, and all that follow must come the same.'[4] To die a good death is the aim of a good life; to be ready for death means to be settled in mind, at peace with the imminent fact of ending and departure. It means to have come to an account with God, acknowledging one's debts in preparation for the ultimate payment of life (*Measure for Measure*, like *Hamlet*, is residually attached to Roman Catholic theology and assumptions):

Angelo	He must die tomorrow.
Isabella	Tomorrow? O, that's sudden! Spare him, spare him!
	He's not prepared for death. Even for our kitchens
	We kill the fowl of season. Shall we serve heaven
	With less respect than we do minister
	To our gross selves?

> (2.2.84–9)

This is the context for the great central scene (3.1) in which Claudio is asked twice, first by the Duke (disguised as a Friar), and then by Isabella, to be prepared to die. The Duke's reasoning is that life is not worth treasuring – because it always and already belongs to death. There should be no fear of death when the passions that make us cling to life are revealed in their true absurdity. Living is already a mode of dying; we already taste life beyond the grave, drawn towards death as to a beckoning finger:

> Merely, thou art death's fool;
> For him thou labour'st by thy flight to shun,

And yet runn'st toward him still.

(3.1.11–13)

The more we are attached to things of this world, the more we are servants of death:

> If thou art rich, thou'rt poor,
> For like an ass whose back with ingots bows,
> Thou bear'st thy heavy riches but a journey,
> And death unloads thee.
>
> (25–8)

The qualities that supposedly honour the living are already undermined, already possessed, by death's poorest agents:

> Thou'rt by no means valiant,
> For thou dost fear the soft and tender fork
> Of a poor worm.
>
> (15–17)

Our sweetest pleasure in an otherwise 'rest'less life is sleep, already a rehearsal of death's peace, if only we knew it:

> Thy best of rest is sleep,
> And that thou oft provok'st, yet grossly fear'st
> Thy death, which is no more.
>
> (17–19)

Even the food that sustains us comes from death, as the grains that feed our livestock, and produce our bread and beer, issue from nothing but the 'dust' of numberless dispersed corpses. But what is still worse, this means we are compounded, grain by grain, of the dead; we do not even possess our own selves:

> Thou art not thyself,
> For thou exist'st on many a thousand grains
> That issue out of dust.
>
> (19–21)

The reason we suffer is that we are not dead. Our bodies are collections of organs whose purpose is to kill the being that hosts them. The horror of illness is not that it curtails pleasure, but that it extends life:

> Friend hast thou none,
> For thine own bowels which do call thee sire,
> The mere effusion of thy proper loins,
> Do curse the gout, serpigo, and the rheum,
> For ending thee no sooner.
>
> (28–32)

The very idea of a purposeful life is a fond illusion, no more than the fumes of bodily digestion. Indeed time itself is a dream, for there is only one moment, one which we are barely even present to experience:

> Thou hast nor youth, nor age,
> But as it were an after-dinner's sleep
> Dreaming on both
>
> (32–4)

The Duke's 'reason' leads to its simple conclusion:

> What's in this
> That bears the name of life? Yet in this life
> Lie hid more thousand deaths; yet death we fear
> That makes these odds all even.
>
> (38–41)

There can be no fear of death once life is exposed as death upon death upon death, a progress of fragments or foretastes of death, waiting for the real thing to cleanse the slate.

The Duke's is perhaps the ultimate speech in Shakespeare expressing the idea of death in life. Life is in hock to death; it is a poor man's death, a suitor for death, hobbled at every step by death. So what on earth is there to fear from the real thing? Here is no Christian comfort, no sense of an afterlife. The Friar's consolation is stoic or classical, even epicurean, rather than Christian. But consider Claudio's response:

> I humbly thank you.
> To sue to live, I find I seek to die,
> And seeking death, find life. Let it come on.
>
> (3.1.41–3)

We might wonder if Claudio has actually been listening to the Friar's tutorial. Instead of stoical acceptance of death, he replies with a proto-Christian hope for redemption in death. The Friar's words hang in the air; they are compelling, even irrefutable – and yet they cannot quite speak to the human specifics of the moment. Cue the re-entrance of Isabella – and with her Claudio's renewed hope of life. In other words, the very moment that Claudio reaches a calm acceptance of death, *drama* intervenes with the rival imperative to desire life.

Philosophical conclusions, in Shakespeare's plays, must always defer to the dynamic metaphysics of theatre, in which the dramatic situation takes precedence over arguments and rationalizations, however logical. Claudius, Hamlet's silkily comforting stepfather, tries to tell the grieving prince that nature's 'common theme / Is death of fathers' (1.2.103–4): 'you must know your father lost a father; / That father lost, lost his' (1.2.89–90). But his argument is irrelevant. Reason is inadequate to emotion, the very stuff of theatre. 'Dispute it like a man', Malcolm clumsily tells Macduff, who has just heard of the massacre of his family on Macbeth's tyrannical order. 'I must also feel it as a man' is the reply (4.3.221–3).

Isabella hopes likewise to persuade her brother to accept death. She will not submit to a 'remedy … to cleave a heart in twain' (3.1.59–60): Angelo's demand that she have sex with him in order to free her brother. 'Better', she tells Angelo, 'it were a brother died at once / Than that a sister, by redeeming him, / Should die forever' (2.4.107–9). It is with these convictions that she approaches her condemned brother:

> Dar'st thou die?
> The sense of death is most in apprehension,
> And the poor beetle that we tread upon
> In corporal sufferance finds a pang as great
> As when a giant dies.
>
> (3.1.75–9)

William Holman Hunt's moralistic Victorian portrait *Claudio and Isabella* pictures the prison encounter between brother and sister (Figure 11). Framed by a window, Claudio, dandily dressed in purple hose and red doublet, looks darkly to the left, fingering the shackles on his ankle. On the right-hand side of the painting the habited Isabella pleads, hands clasped. The light falls on her face while Claudio's is in shadow: her upright demeanour contrasts, visually and morally, with his slouch. But the play itself makes their meeting much more ethically ambiguous.

Claudio's initial resolution is reassuringly textbook, giving a romantic tinge to the play's repeated association of death and sex:

> If I must die,
> I will encounter darkness as a bride,
> And hug it in mine arms.
>
> (3.1.81–3)

Characteristically, Isabella's response is at once literal and ecstatic – and in this very absoluteness stunningly imaginative. She seems to take his cliché as a time-erasing

Figure 11 Holman Hunt's image of the encounter between Claudio and Isabella from *Measure for Measure* seems to make her a beacon of light in the prison, but the play stages a more uncomfortable meeting from which the siblings are never allowed to recover. William Holman Hunt, *Claudio and Isabella*, 1850. Tate Britain/© The Print Collector/Alamy

actuality: she hears her brother, and sees in her mind's eye their parents coupling in the dark; Claudio's bride of 'darkness' turns from death, into his mother, and then back into the death for which his proof of fidelity to his sister makes him fit; he becomes one with his father, both in the act of conceiving his own life (Claudio is as though born again at this moment of recognition) and in the fact of that life's ending. Truly, in the rapturous, cloistered, sacrificial imagination of Isabella, we are born to die:

> There spake my brother; there my father's grave
> Did utter forth a voice.
>
> (84–5)

To his wishful sister, he has already entered death. His is a voice from beyond the grave. She would bless him and bid him precipitous farewell, and then rush from this hideous prison-limbo back into her own secluded cell. But Claudio is not ready to be a memorial. Humans are passionate animals; and passion clings to the body, however degraded, and to the singular mind and soul we have always known; and with these attachments comes once more the dread of what lies beyond:

> *Claudio*   Death is a fearful thing.
> *Isabella*   And shamèd life a hateful.
> *Claudio*   Ay, but to die, and go we know not where;
> To lie in cold obstruction, and to rot;
> This sensible warm motion to become
> A kneaded clod
>
> (117–21)

Figure 12 Frontispiece from Thomas Fuller's seventeenth-century collection of biographies of divines and religious men. *Abel Redevivus, or, The dead yet speaking,* 1652 Bodleian Library, Wood 352.

Robert Watson has written about the underside of assured religious assertions of salvation, visible when early modern culture gives way to 'repressed anxieties about death as eternal annihilation': 'these dark constellations create a sinister gravity which constantly threatens to topple the confident Christian stance'.⁵ Here

ABEL REDEVIVUS
or
The dead yet speaking
By T. Fuller and other
Eminent Divines.

Mors vltima linea rerum est

Nunc levior cippus non imprimit oßa!
laudat posteritas, nunc non e manibus illis
Nunc non e tumulo fortunaque favilla
Nascuntur viola! Perſ. Sat.1.37

Sould by Iohn Stafford at the George at Fleete bridge 1652 Ro: Vaughan ſculp:

in *Measure for Measure* those anxieties are laid bare: annihilation replaces salvation as the keynote of mortality. The sentence Claudio speaks is horribly final, ending with the utter self-loss of a 'kneaded clod'. But a rival teleology attaches to the *line*: each line is a life-thought, each subtly different, vacillating between finality and uncertainty, putrefaction and mental wonder. This suggests why Claudio *cannot* end here. To be a 'kneaded clod' is in fact unthinkable. And so Claudio at once recharges himself – no less dreadfully, but animated by its own terror – with thoughts of the undead spirit:

> and the delighted spirit
> To bathe in fiery floods, or to reside
> In thrilling region of thick-ribbèd ice;
> To be imprisoned in the viewless winds,
> And blown with restless violence round about
> The pendent world; or to be worse than worst
> Of those that lawless and incertain thought
> Imagine howling – 'tis too horrible!

> (3.1.121–8)

In part the vision (for all its poetic vividness) is formulaic, as Claudio imagines himself tossed and blown through the proverbial horror-scapes of limbo or hell. But this physical geography – ice, fire, wind – does not really define Shakespeare's view of being dead. It isn't the nouns, the would-be known things, that define this vision. Unusually for Shakespeare, it isn't even really the verbs, as much as they capture death's mix of confinement and swooning unfreedom. The defining thing is the adjectives that modify this movement – or, perhaps more to the point, that modify the attempt to imagine it: *fiery, thrilling, viewless, restless, lawless, incertain, horrible*.

The region is 'thrilling', a word that means various pertinent things: to move with sudden emotion; to pierce or penetrate; and to enthral like a slave or prisoner. This evokes the dizzying paroxysm of imagining being dead, the individual at once stunned and stabbed and bound. Then follow the three self-voiding nouns, *view-*

less, *restless*, *lawless*: death is a state of negation, of withdrawal. The most telling word here is 'viewless' – meaning to be either blind or invisible, and applying both to the thing not seen (the winds) and the thing not seeing (the 'delighted spirit'). All is occlusion: not only the subject individual, but nature itself is in a state of possible shut-down, working invisibly beyond an invisible wall, never to be known (the same applies to 'fiery', which demolishes even as it illuminates).

This horrid vertiginous thinking culminates – and is suddenly arrested – with the final vision of 'those that lawless and incertain thought / Imagine howling'. Once again the language is disorientating. It is ambiguous whether Claudio's 'thought' is lawless and incertain, transgressing as it does all boundaries, rules and verifications; or whether it is 'those' he imagines 'howling' in their undead despair. The answer, again, is both: and it is precisely in this ambiguity that we find the 'viewless', 'restless', 'lawless' truth of death as Shakespeare sees it.

Death both provokes and baffles the imagination. It levels the distinction between oneself and others, and between imagined and actual worlds. There is no longer a separation of thought and fact, now and then, or is and if. What else to do but try to shake one's head and *refuse* the thought?

However, Claudio's escape from death is in name only. His plea for his life in exchange for his sister's virginity receives from her a withering reply:

> Thy sin's not accidental, but a trade. …
> 'Tis best that thou diest quickly.
>
> (3.1.151–3)

A fierce dismissal that is quickly followed by the Friar's renewed attempt to prepare the sinner for death:

> Do not satisfy your resolution with hopes that are fallible. Tomorrow you must die. Go to
>   your knees and make ready.
>
> (3.1.170–72)

Ashamed and chastened, Claudio surrenders: 'I am so out of love with life that I will sue to be rid of it' (173–4). And so he leaves, a truth in his ears that not even comedy can allay: *tomorrow you must die*.

The shadowy double of Claudio is Barnardine, a prisoner who for years has been on death row, and who is called by Angelo to be executed on the same afternoon. But Barnardine's is no ordinary death sentence. He has many times been given leave to escape, but does not. Likewise he has many times been called to execution, the warrant in his gaoler's hand, but this too has not moved him. His guilt is 'manifest', and 'not denied by himself' – not denied, but not confirmed either. Barnardine, drinking away his days, exists in just such a limbo: imprisoned but not strictly under arrest; held by law but not answerable to it; guilty but unconfessing. The Duke hears of his case, and decides on an elegant stratagem. He will swap Barnardine's head for Claudio's, deliver it to Angelo, and doubly serve justice and comic lore. Claudio will be saved, Angelo set up for punishment, and the unregenerate Barnardine sacrificed.

In his guise as the Friar, the Duke goes to Barnardine to 'give him a present shrift, and advise him for a better place'. In other words, to prepare Barnardine for death. But it doesn't work out as he plans:

Duke	Sir, induced by my charity, and hearing how hastily you are to depart, I am come to advise you, comfort you, and pray with you.
Barnardine	Friar, not I. I have been drinking hard all night, and I will have more time to prepare me, or they shall beat out my brains with billets. I will not consent to die this day, that's certain.
Duke	Oh sir, you must; and therefore, I beseech you, Look forward on the journey you shall go.
Barnardine	I swear I will not die today, for any man's persuasion.
Duke	But hear you –
Barnardine	Not a word. If you have anything to say to me, come to my ward, for thence will not I today.
Exit	
Enter Provost	

Duke	Unfit to live or die. Oh gravel heart!
	(4.3.47–61)

Various things are happening here. Shakespeare is clearly teasing with the morality play tradition that underpins *Measure for Measure*. The 'Friar' is a heavenly summoner – 'Look you, sir, here comes your ghostly father' (4.3.45–6) – calling the condemned everyman to death. But the man simply refuses to come. In this play-world, death will indeed be delayed. The absolute modal verbs of the Duke, so appropriate to death – 'you must', 'you shall' – defer to the prisoner's 'will'. The terrible injunction of the morality play *Everyman* – there can be no delaying, no tarrying; you *shall* die when death calls, and the call is sudden – is defied by the simple caprice of a hungover nobody.

Barnardine is no doubt depraved, perverse and nihilistic. But his subversive resistance of due process is also thrilling. Lurking in the margins, stinking in his straw, he becomes a kind of pioneering everyman, risking the defiance that the rest of us can only dream of – and, what is better, succeeding. 'I swear I will not die today on any man's persuasion', he says: and he does not. There is a curious integrity in his defiance, in the way he sticks so stubbornly to type: and it is perhaps the integrity of theatre. Barnardine lives both under the eternal mark of death, and in a half-lit, magically protected limbo where death *cannot* reach. Barnardine becomes a talisman of Shakespeare's own primary commitment: to the synthetic lore of the stage rather than the mortal law of the human body.

Hence the way Barnardine's refusal to die gives way to a brazen piece of improvised theatrical machinery. Barnardine is 'unprepared, unmeet for death' – but serendipitously 'There died this morning … One Ragozine, a most notorious pirate', whose 'beard and head' happen to be the spitting image of Claudio's, 'Just of his colour' (4.3.64–70). Comic substitution allays actual death: 'Oh, 'tis an accident that heaven provides' (74). And in a jiffy the pirate's head is carried triumphantly onto the stage. Death is 'transported' into a blatant prop – and the invincible Barnardine survives to play another day.

Figure 13 This picture of John Donne, the poet and Dean of St Paul's Cathedral, 'muffled' in his shroud, was commissioned by him as a *memento mori*. He had himself dressed in a winding-sheet, and posed with his eyes closed, to anticipate the way he expected to look when called to the Last Judgement. It is placed here as a frontispiece to the publication of a sermon that Donne delivered a few weeks before his death in 1631. This image provided the model for his tomb in St Paul's Cathedral. *Death's Duel*, J. Donne, 1633. Reproduced by kind permission of the Principal and Fellows of Brasenose College, Oxford.

DEATHS
DVELL,
OR,

A Consolation to the Soule, againſt
the dying Life, and liuing
Death of the Body.

Deliuered in a Sermon at White Hall, before the
KINGS MAIESTY, *in the beginning*
of Lent, 1630.

. By that late learned and Reuerend Diuine,
IOHN DONNE, Dr. in Diuinity,
& Deane of S.*Pauls*, London.
Being his laſt Sermon, and called by his Maieſties houſhold
THE DOCTORS OWNE FVNERALL SERMON.

LONDON,
Printed by THOMAS HARPER, for *Richard Redmer*
and *Beniamin Fiſher*, and are to be ſold at the ſigne
of the Talbot in Alderſ-gate ſtreet.
M.DC.XXXII.

Measure for Measure displaces the actuality of death onto a prop. But the play-world never escapes death's mark, even as it goes through the motions of doing so. Claudio, for example, does not speak again after the horrors of the prison scene. His subsequent role in the play is akin to that of mute revenant or ghost. His appearance in the final scene, 'muffled', makes him a kind of troubled Lazarus, another brother returned from the grave. Symbolically Claudio enters wrapped in his own grave-clothes, like the image of John Donne in his winding sheet in the book of his dying sermon, *Death's Duel* (Figure 13). Before he can be reunited with his lover Juliet, he must meet again the sister who has so fiercely condemned him. And they are reunited in a passage of the darkest ambiguity: just as Angelo would have exchanged Claudio's life for Isabella's body, the Duke would now swap Claudio's life – returned from the presumed-dead – for Isabella's hand in marriage:

If he be like your brother, for his sake
Is he pardoned; and for your lovely sake
Give me your hand, and say you will be mine.

(5.1.489–91)

She says nothing, either to the Duke or her brother; Claudio and Juliet are likewise mute. His reunion with the pregnant Juliet is sometimes presented in rose-tinted productions as a wordless ecstasy. However, there is no liberation here from death's exchanges; everything remains fatally contingent:

Whom he begot with child, let her appear,
And he shall marry her. The nuptial finished,
Let him be whipped and hanged.

(510–12)

The Duke passes sentence here on the roguish Lucio – but the words are magnetically choric, and speak just as much to the terrible contract that Claudio continues to endure: you love with your life. The stage at play's end is crowded with

ufer quomam exaudiet
dominus vorem oronis mee
Quia metinauit do
minus aurem suam michi et in die

the guilty and condemned: Angelo, Lucio, Claudio, Barnardine – even Isabella, standing silent in the glare of the Duke's unsought proposal, pointing at her like death's bone. Each figure is the others' shadow. There is remission from sentence, but no ultimate release:

> 'An Angelo for Claudio, death for death'.
> Haste still pays haste, and leisure answers leisure;
> Like doth quit like, and *MEASURE* still for *MEASURE*.
>
> (5.1.406–8)

Measure for Measure is an early example of tragicomedy, a new kind of play that pivoted on the simultaneous proximity and avoidance of death. Shakespeare's later collaborator John Fletcher defined it like this: 'not so called in respect of mirth and killing, but in respect it wants deaths, which is enough to make it no tragedy, yet brings some near it, which is enough to make it no comedy'.[6] Nineteenth-century scholars coined the term 'problem play' for this and other uncomfortable 'comedies', such as *Troilus and Cressida*, *All's Well that Ends Well*, and even *Hamlet*. Although, given the persisting stench of death in all of them – a savour that lingers beyond their ambivalent ends – perhaps they would be better termed *comi-tragedies*.

3
Death in Comedy

He shall not die

(The Comedy of Errors, 5.1.133)

Comedy, we tend to think, is a death-free zone.
But consider this:

> Proceed, Solinus, to procure my fall,
> And by the doom of death end woes and all.

(The Comedy of Errors, 1.1.1–2)

So begins Shakespeare's first great farce. The speaker is Egeon, a merchant of Syracuse, who has made the mistake of arriving at the enemy bay of Ephesus. To do so is to die – unless a thousand marks can be raised to quit the penalty and 'ransom' the poor merchant free. He is granted a day's grace for the money to be found, and exits:

> Hopeless and helpless doth Egeon wend,
> But to procrastinate his lifeless end.

> (1.1.157–8)

Death is put on hold while the entertainment begins; to 'procrastinate' means to suspend until the next day. Comedy is all about youthful play, non-fatal mistakes, and the avoiding, delaying or forgetting of death.

Figure 15 Like the ring (Figure 3), this seventeenth-century watch case decorated with a human skull is a powerful *memento mori*: time ticks to our deaths. In *Twelfth Night* Malvolio fantasises about owning a watch as a mark of his elevated status, but the whole play is preoccupied with what Olivia calls 'the waste of time' (3.1.129). WA.1947.191.58 © Ashmolean Museum, University of Oxford.

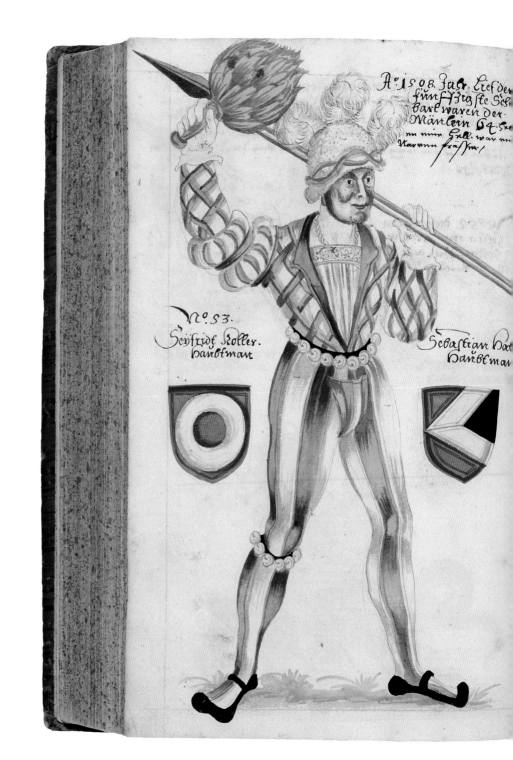

Figures 16 and 17 Carnival festivity is often marked with the iconography of Death in more antic form: Death as the jester. Sometimes the frantic energy of carnival and its etymological associations with meat and killing slide into anxiety as the clock runs down. Bodleian Library, MS. Douce 346, fols 240v–241r and 245v–246r (a *Schembartbuch*, an illustrated account *c.* 1640 of the former annual procession of the butchers' guild at Nuremberg).

Anno 1508 Jahr Lief der Fünff grösste Schembart
war. Seyfridt Rallur unnd Sebastian Hallur Haubt.
leuth ni Schaubaut waren der Mänlein 64 ni weiß
braun unnd grün, unnd liefen auf der Ennm durch
Stuben auf der wag auß Enstunden in dan den Metzgern
fuelßlike.

Nr° 3. diese zweer Schembarts Haubtman.
hetten eine Sel war ein schloß auf einer.
Vielleichten daraust sauß ein großer Man und mol
halb gattun höch. Der fraß Kinder nineß nach den
Andren. daß gab mir großes gelaichter. unnd mir
große freust untrer die klein Kinder. wurd am
Leßtern mit nach voz den Rathauß gestürmt Nnnd
Umprandt/ Ju diesen Jahr war doß Fastla nit.

Er unnd der Herzog Friedereß Ennsst Gubernator/
Jun diesen Jahr fing Kai: Mapmilliane nin Krieg
mit denen Unnedigern an/

A:.1513 Fahr. lief der Fürst
funffzigste Bambart. war
der Man lein 39

N:o 8
Bieronimus·
Pessler·
Hauptman

.58. war hieronimus Keßler Haubtman
schönbart vnnd warun der Männlein 39 ni
i farb gekleidet. vnnd liß Ihn auß Inn Hainzla
Roßmann ß inß Hauß dier 4 Häuß bestunden
von dem katzenn vmb 12 fl. vnnd gab ein Mann
ein schambart. 3 fl. vnnd die hell war ein Hauß
d Inn Das lochen mit Narrenn. Die man.
schüß vnnd Büchß für herauß. Der Norren
kochen hinß. wie Ihr Mann in schambart be klai
ist hetten Viel kurzweil mit Ihnen. wirdt
Lehre mit wachen vor dem Rathhauß zu
schnelt vnnd vm prandt.

But there is more to death in comedy than this. The fact or fear of death is the spur to life, the necessary counter that gives tension and energy to the action. Death provides a formal frame establishing the boundaries of the game. Without it the action would be lax, there would be too much choice, too much time, like tennis without a net. It gives the story and jokes their compulsion, edge and timing. Comedy must always be up against it, harried and pressed and working in tiny circles, the threat of loss or failure ever present. The clock is running out on festivity:

> The capon burns, the pig falls from the spit.
> The clock hath strucken twelve upon the bell
>
> (1.2.44–5)

Comedy cannot be comfortable either with elongated time, or (which is much the same thing) with extinction.

This is why death seems always to hang over Shakespeare's comedies. In *A Midsummer Night's Dream*, having heard how Theseus won Hippolyta's love 'doing thee injuries', the unhappy father Egeus enters, insisting on his right to 'dispose' of his daughter Hermia as he wishes, either to the gentleman of his choice 'Or to her death' (1.1.42–4). In *As You Like It* the heroine Rosalind is banished from the court on pain of death, her fault being that she is her father's daughter. *Much Ado About Nothing* opens with the gentleman fresh from war, tabulating the dead, and there is a sense throughout the play that the men's cruel and mirthless games are somehow licensed by the killing they have witnessed. *The Merchant of Venice* begins with the 'sad' Antonio, his mind tossing on the ocean where his richly laden ships are precariously afloat – headed, we already surmise, to destruction. *Twelfth Night* starts with the shipwreck already accomplished, and the travails of the heroine Viola shadowed by fears that her twin brother is dead – just as her fellow heroine, Olivia, is deep in morbid mourning for her recently deceased brother. All this before we even get to the supposedly darker comedies that take

Figure 18 One early audience member thought that Olivia in *Twelfth Night* was a widow: the imagery of female mourning was strongly associated with widowhood, although in the play it is her father and brother that Olivia remembers. A lady in black, dated Venice 1591, from the *Album Amicorum* of Jan van der Deck (MS. Rawl. B. 21, fol. 45r).

Un buon caúallo, o mal caúallo vúole ún sperone:
Una buona donna, o mala donna vúol ún bastone.
Ospitulandum amicis:
U. A. A.

Amico súo amicæ recordationis
ergó scribebat hac A.f.w.c.
cIꝺ Iꝺ XCI. d. 23. Maji.
Fridrich Von Rosstodt
Venetiis.

over from Shakespeare's mid-career. The action of *Measure for Measure* swings upon the death sentence dealt young Claudio for having sex with his betrothed before marrying. *All's Well That Ends Well* is even more death-haunted. 'In delivering my son from me I bury a second husband', says the Countess in the play's dizzying first words, turning birth (delivery) into burial and mourning into a kind of emotional tarbrush, blackening every act and emotion with its taint.

Comedy may be an interlude between the oblivions of past and future, just as a play is an interlude between responsibilities – a bit of time off. But the escape is neither free nor restful, and always overshadowed by the facts it would forget:

> Sweet recreation barred, what doth ensue
> But moody and dull melancholy,
> Kinsman to grim and comfortless despair,
> And at her heels a huge infectious troop
> Of pale distemperatures and foes to life?
>
> (*The Comedy of Errors*, 5.1.79–83)

The mad world of comedy is right next door to the place of execution; the clock ticks, and death awaits.

> *Merchant*   By this, I think, the dial point's at five.
> Anon, I'm sure, the Duke himself in person
> Comes this way to the melancholy vale,
> The place of death and sorry execution,
> Behind the ditches of the abbey here.
>
> (5.1.119–23)

Death might be lurking anywhere; it takes the most hideous disguises.

Marry, sir, she's the kitchen wench, and all grease; and I know not what use to put her to but to make a lamp of her, and run from her by her own light. I warrant her rags and the tallow in them will burn a Poland winter. If she lives till doomsday, she'll burn a week longer than the whole world.

(3.2.96–101)

The world of comedy is turned upside down. In this it intensifies the basic geography of the playhouses – situated in the 'liberties' of London, beyond the walls of the city's jurisdiction. But with freedom come fear and surprise; you'd better watch your back. The town of Ephesus is full of 'Soul-killing witches that deform the body', and 'many suchlike liberties of sin' (1.2.100–102). The setting is nominally a street or house, but it is also a garish underworld in which signs of beauty are beckoners of death. As Antipholus S. says, feeling himself bewitched by the sister of the woman who claims she is his wife, 'But lest myself be guilty to self-wrong, / I'll stop mine ears against the mermaid's song' (3.2. 169–70). He fears that the sister is a siren, drawing him to destruction. Characters repeatedly think they are in some kind of hell, full of devils, sorcerers, and shape-shifters:

Adriana	Where is thy master, Dromio? Is he well?
Dromio S.	No, he's in Tartar limbo, worse than hell.
	A devil in an everlasting garment hath him,
	One whose hard heart is buttoned up with steel;
	A fiend, a fairy, pitiless and rough;
	A wolf, nay worse, a fellow all in buff;
	A back-friend, a shoulder-clapper, one that countermands
	The passages of alleys, creeks, and narrow lands;
	A hound that runs counter, and yet draws dryfoot well,
	One that, before the Judgement, carries poor souls to hell.

(4.2.31–40)

Dromio is referring to the arrest by a sergeant of the man he wrongly believes is his master. But more profoundly this world is a version of hell, where no one and nothing can be trusted, where no one is who others think they are – so much so that they begin to doubt their own identity. The town becomes a 'limbo', in which

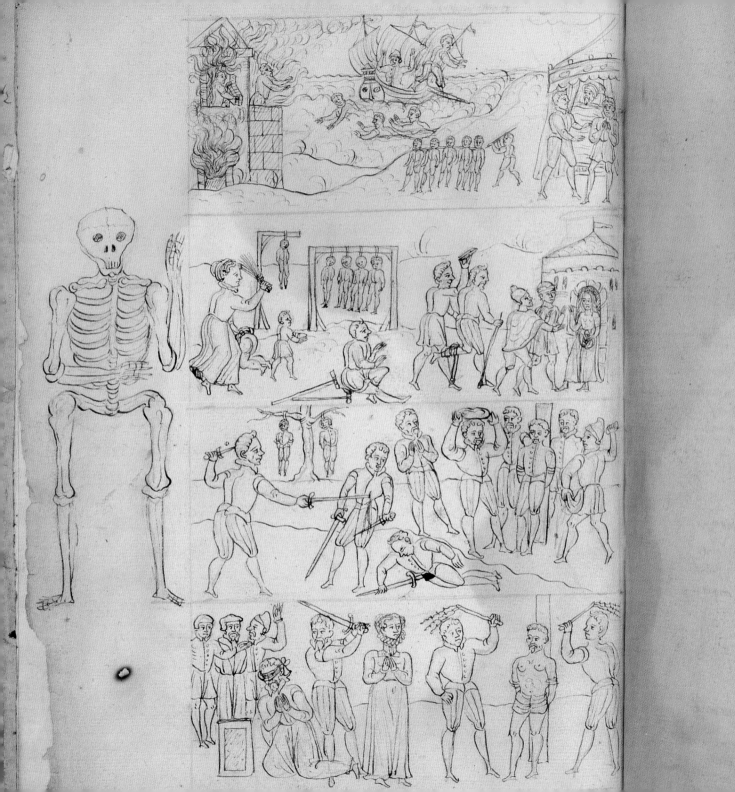

there is nothing but dangerous byways between living and death, homelessness and safety, a place mapped by 'passages of alleys, creeks and narrow lands', where the very environment closes in and contracts, where you are followed by a 'hound that runs counter', the sniffing devil, such that whichever way you turn there he is, pinching you to account before you are ready. Dromio evokes a place of terrifying un-freedom. The constant fear is arrest – not by a constable who takes you to prison, but by the sergeant Death, who takes you 'before the Judgement' – without any reckoning, without the chance to clear one's slate – down to hell. Dromio calls this sergeant by a series of titles, some of them conventional names for devils and destroyers – fiend, fairy, wolf. But he is also a shoulder-clapper – both a policeman arresting you in your tracks, and an insinuating friend, seducing you into your destruction. In this 'Tartar limbo' the poor soul doesn't know which way to turn. Every unknown face might be the demon. At one moment the devil who 'hath him' is dressed in steel, which then becomes 'an everlasting garment', like a coffin or a burial shroud; then the devil is a 'fellow all in buff', both the leather of the sergeant and the awful image of the naked body, the flesh stripped of all protection, all illusion, as life is reduced to the basic contract: he becomes the grinning skeleton, dancing the dance of death.

A moment later a beautiful woman appears:

Antipholus S. Satan, avoid! I charge thee, tempt me not!
Dromio S. Master, is this Mistress Satan?
Antipholus S. It is the devil.
Dromio S. Nay, she is worse, she is the devil's dam; and here she comes in the habit of a light wench… It is written they appear to men like angels of light. Light is an effect of fire, and fire will burn. Ergo, light wenches will burn. Come not near her.

(4.3.48–57)

To touch this 'light', sexually enticing wench is to risk both the burning pains of venereal disease and the everlasting fires of hell. If this horror is partially

Figure 19 The skeleton presides over various scenes of early modern death in this miscellany of religious verse and prose: at sea, on the gallows, in combat, and by torture. Commonplace book of Sir Alexander Colepeper, *c.* 1600–1616: Bodleian Library, MS. Tanner 118, fol. 20v.

redeemed by our awareness that the characters are mired in error, it is precisely these errors that reveal people as they *are*, without the protection of custom and normality. By the same logic, it might be the terrifying truth beneath the social surface. The world of comedy works like a hologram.

> *Dromio E.*   Mistress, *respice finem* – respect your end – or rather, to prophesy like the parrot, 'Beware the rope's end'.
>
> (4.4.42–4)

In some ways the resident genius of *The Comedy of Errors* is the 'doting wizard', Doctor Pinch. Like everything in this play-world, he is double. Looked at with one eye, he is a trembling, ecstatic, saffron-faced old conjurer; looked at with the other eye, he is Death itself:

> A mere anatomy, a mountebank,
> A threadbare juggler and a fortune-teller,
> A needy, hollow-eyed, sharp-looking-wretch,
> A living dead man.
>
> (5.1.239–42)

Death has many disguises, but the skull is behind them all:

> And gazing in mine eyes, feeling my pulse,
> And with no face (as 'twere) outfacing me,
> Cries out I was possessed.
>
> (244–6)

Pinch seeks to exorcise the devil from the twins:

> I charge thee, Satan, housed within this man,
> To yield possession to my holy prayers,
> And to thy state of darkness hie thee straight …

> Mistress, both man and master is possessed,
> I know it by their pale and deadly looks.
> They must be bound and laid in some dark room.
>
> $$(4.4.55-7, 93-5)$$

To be bound in darkness is more than a way of purging the devil. It is to suffer the baffling illogic, the loss of boundaries, of life beyond life:

> They fell upon me, bound me, bore me thence,
> And in a dark and dankish vault at home
> There left me and my man, both bound together,
> Till, gnawing with my teeth my bonds in sunder,
> I gain'd my freedom
>
> $$(5.1.247-51)$$

It is a simulation of death. But notice how it also a recollection of *not* being-born – of being trapped in the womb with one's twin. The unborn boy bites the cord and gets free: and then a moment later we hear how in this act, having escaped the dank vault, he also freed his slave, Dromio.

This is the true dream of comedy: 'Graves yawn, and yield your dead' (*Much Ado About Nothing*, 5.3.19). It is a rehearsal of death; a limbo or oblivion that can be suffered and yet escaped; a swooning inoculation against the great killer. This is why the play's final scene goes on to bring brothers, fathers and mothers back from death into life, making the dead speak and move. Each of the twins in fact has a brother; the husband has a living wife, the wife a husband. From death comes birth.

Death bares its teeth in more menacing ways in *The Merchant of Venice*, a comedy in which each action is a perilous risk, a conscious gamble in which the stakes are pretty much everything. It is built upon a great principle of Shakespearean drama – that the smallest thing, the most commonplace event, might generate thoughts of catastrophe:

Figure 20 Dance of death imagery adorns the margins of this sixteenth-century French Book of Hours. Bodleian Library, MS. Douce 135, fols 72v–73r

Omine deduc me in iusticia tua propt'
inimicos meos dirige in conspectu tuo viam
meam.

m non est in ore eorum veritas cor eo$\bar{r}$c.
vanum est.

epulchrum patens est guttur eorum li
quis suis dolose agebãt, iudica illos deus.

ecidant a cogitationibus suis secundum
multitudinem impietatum eorum expelle e
os qm irritauerunt te dñe.

t letentur omnes qui sperant in te in eter
num: exultabunt & habitabis in eis.

t gloriabuntur in te oñis qui diligunt
nomen tuum: qm tu benedices iusto.

omine vt scuto: bone voluntatis tue co
ronasti nos.

equiem. Añ. Dirige domine deus me^9
in conspectu tuo viam meã. Añ. Conuertere.

Omine ne in furore tuo arguas me:
neqz in ira tua corripias me.

iserere mei domine qm infirmus sum.
sana me dñe qm conturbata sunt ossa mea.
t anima mea turbata est valde: sed tu
dñe usqz quo.

ARCHIEPISCO
PVS

My wind cooling my broth
Would blow me to an ague when I thought
What harm a wind too great might do at sea.

(1.1.22–4)

The other side of this sort of thinking is that anything – a simple object, a meta-phor – can stand for the biggest questions of life and of death. Comedy allows the simple thing to be simple, the homely thing to be homely – but it also knows that if we look with sharper eyes we might see something much darker and stranger. As the clown Lancelot Gobbo has it, 'The fiend is at mine elbow and tempts me' (2.2.2–3) – even if the thing we *see* at his elbow is a pot of beer.

Antonio's entire fortune is at sea, his treasure deep in the innards of various ships. None arrives safely home. The ships become coffins. Likewise, the heroine Portia's fortune is locked in one of three caskets, as determined by the dying wish of her father. Whoever opens the one with her portrait in it will take her and all she owns. Each casket, like each of Antonio's doomed ships, contains in miniature the principles of this play-world.

The Moroccan prince chooses the golden casket and finds in it a skull: 'A carrion death, within whose empty eye / There is a written scroll' carrying the terse message that 'All that glisters is not gold; … Gilded tombs do worms infold' (2.7.63–9). The Prince of Aragon opens the silver casket and gets as his reward a fool's head: 'Take what wife you will to bed, / I will ever be your head. / So be gone; you are sped' (2.9.69–71). The moralizing skull is one side of comic risk; the garish, smiling fool is the other. Each is a death sentence. The two unwanted heads work like a comic Janus: whichever way you face, which ever face you see, the other is always lurking, at any moment liable to turn into your mirror.

When Portia's beloved Bassanio enters to make his choice of casket, we may assume that we have entered the world of romance, where such errors are banished. In some ways this is true. He chooses the correct lead casket and discovers inside 'the fair Portia's counterfeit'. Death and folly are replaced by fairness. But the

Figure 21 The playgoer, astrologer and physician Simon Forman was often consulted about whether absent individuals were alive or dead. This image from his earliest casebook shows astrological charts drawn in response to an enquiry by Margaret Bateman about her husband who had gone to sea and not returned. A week later, Forman did a reading for 'Mary Ratlif', aged 17, who wanted to know the fate of Henry Hurleston, after 'he went to Sea with Sir fraonces Drak'. Bodleian Library, MS. Ashmole 234, fol. 37r.

Jone Bromiale of 29 yeare
1596 ... 13 ... ...
... 30 ... ...
...

Margaret Coulie
... 1596 ...
...

Margaret Bateman
... 1596 ...
...

Jeane Turner of
40 yeares of her birth 1596
... ... at 30 ...
...

Josep Paine ... buckle
of 30 yeares 1596 ... 13 ...

Edith Midwich of
... in bissops ...
... 1596 ... 13 ...

... Annes of 50 yeares of
age ... 1596 ...

whole theme of the casket scenes has been the danger of judging by appearances, and so it is here. Perhaps the most striking example is Portia's golden hair. These gorgeous locks were evoked in the play's very first 'picturing' of Portia:

> In Belmont is a lady richly left,
> And she is fair…
> For the four winds blow in from every coast
> Renownèd suitors, and her sunny locks
> Hang on her temples like a golden fleece
>
> (1.1.161–70)

She is lovely, and rich, with golden locks that the winds compete to bless. Bassanio wagers his friend's life to gain access. But now see what becomes of this hair in the casket scene, as Bassanio studies her portrait:

> Here in her hairs
> The painter plays the spider, and hath woven
> A golden mesh t'untrap the hearts of men
> Faster than gnats in cobwebs.
>
> (3.2.120–23)

Beauty traps, tortures and swiftly kills. The prize of the leaden casket ironically confirms what Bassanio had a moment ago reasoned about the dangerous allure of the golden casket.

> Look on beauty,
> And you shall see 'tis purchased by the weight,
> Which therein works a miracle in nature,
> Making them lightest that wear most of it.
> So are those crisped, snaky, golden locks
> Which makes such wanton gambols with the wind
> Upon supposed fairness, often known

To be the dowry of a second head,
The skull that bred them in the sepulchre.
Thus ornament is but the guiled shore
To a most dangerous sea

(3.2.88–98)

Bassanio is imagining a golden wig, stitched together from the hair of a dead woman and now adorning the head of some 'supposèd' living beauty. Like sirens in romances, the hair gambols with the wind, seeming to dance and sing, as from their 'guilèd shore' they beckon men to the 'dangerous sea' of man-swallowing female sex. The 'miracle' of beauty is a nauseating fraud, 'crispèd' and 'snaky' as though fresh from hell's oily furnace. As with the 'counterfeit' picture of Portia, art itself is in commerce with death.

Bassanio wants to distinguish true from feigned beauty, the living from the dead. However, to do so is no easier – perhaps no more possible – than to distinguish true from feigned art. This is why Shakespeare's language is so dense with interconnections. The 'dowry of a second head' in part refers to the dead woman whose hair has been shaved and sold (death as a kind of second marriage contract). But the 'second head' also belongs to the woman wearing the wig. This is partly because another's head supplements her own; partly because this second head that she wears (itself born from death) looks ahead to her own death and the 'dowry' that she will then pay – nothing else but her 'skull'. The 'second head' becomes her ghostly accompaniment, tracing her every 'wanton gambol'. But it is also her own 'skull', ineradicably *there* whatever her golden locks like to pretend. As Portia herself says, 'I stand for sacrifice' (3.2.57). At every point along this chain of substitutes – creditors and debtors, suitors and sought, torturers and tortured, skulls, fools and fair ladies – life is on the line.

This is evident from a single epitomizing line: 'The skull that bred them in the sepulchre'. It is a grotesque image of a single skull – a mother skull like some foul Error Monster, venting human forms from deep inside the dank soil and rank air

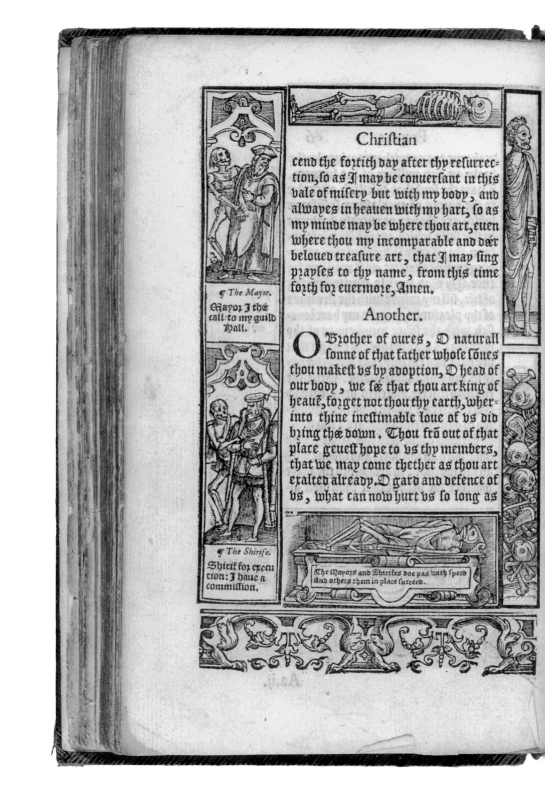

Christian

cend the fortith day after thy resurrec=
tion, so as I may be conuersant in this
vale of misery but with my body, and
alwayes in heauen with my hart, so as
my minde may be where thou art, euen
where thou my incomparable and dær
beloued treasure art, that I may sing
prayses to thy name, from this time
forth for euermore, Amen.

Another.

O Brother of oures, O naturall
sonne of that father whose sones
thou makest vs by adoption, O head of
our body, we sæ that thou art king of
heauē, forget not thou thy earth, wher=
into thine inestimable loue of vs did
bring thæ down. Thou frō out of that
place geuest hope to vs thy members,
that we may come thether as thou art
exalted already. O gard and defence of
vs, what can now hurt vs so long as

The Mayor.
Mayor: I thæ
call to my guild
hall.

The Shirife.
Shirif for execu
tion: I haue a
commission.

The Mayors and Shirifes doe pas with speed
And others them in place succeed.

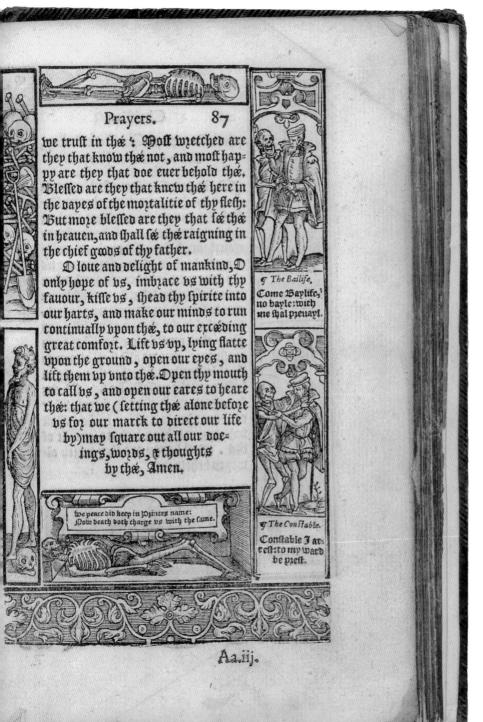

we truſt in thæ: Moſt wretched are
they that know thæ not, and moſt happy are they that doe euer behold thæ.
Bleſſed are they that knew thæ here in
the dayes of the moꝛtalitie of thy fleſh:
But moꝛe bleſſed are they that ſæ thæ
in heauen, and ſhall ſæ thæ raigning in
the chief gœds of thy father.

O loue and delight of mankind, O
only hope of vs, imbꝛace vs with thy
fauour, kiſſe vs, ſhead thy ſpirite into
our harts, and make our minds to run
continually vpon thæ, to our excæding
great comfoꝛt. Lift vs vp, lying flatte
vpon the ground, open our eyes, and
lift them vp vnto thæ. Open thy mouth
to call vs, and open our eares to heare
thæ: that we (ſetting thæ alone befoꝛe
vs foꝛ our marck to direct our life
by) may ſquare out all our doe-
ings, woꝛds, & thoughts
by thæ, Amen.

We peace did keep in Pꝛinces name:
Now death doth charge vs with the ſame.

❡ The Bailiſe.

Come Baylife,
no bayle: with
me ſhal pꝛeuayl.

❡ The Conſtable.

Conſtable I ar-
reſt: to my ward
be pꝛeſt.

of the tomb. Each individual skull is a repetition of this original one – including the heads in Portia's caskets. The nightmare logic of this vision therefore passes into the hidden heads in each casket – each casket, of course, becoming another kind of 'sepulchre' or burial place. One casket has a skull, the next a fool's head, the next a counterfeit of female beauty. Each is the ghostly 'second head' of the other; each the other's 'dowry'.

Language here performs the role of the great leveller, death. Bassanio's speech draws together various of the play's preoccupations, finding one inside the other, or making one give birth to the other. Conventional distinctions disappear between human and non-human, eroticism and commercialism, beauty and foulness, life and death.

But this is not the end of the deathly substitutions. At every point Bassanio recalls the fatal 'hazards', the dicing with death, which got him entrance into Portia's chamber in the first place: that is, his friend Antonio's 'bond' with Shylock. His speech implicitly evokes Antonio's ships, laden heavily with treasure ('purchased by the weight') as they plough the waves, the prows of the boats decked with wooden sculptures of ladies with flowing hair, making 'wanton gambols' with the 'supposed fairness' of 'the wind'.

Everything for which Bassanio longs hangs upon these winds staying fair. But as we already know – and Bassanio only now finds out – Antonio's ships have been 'wrecked on the narrow seas', and now 'like carcasses … lie buried' (3.1.3–6). Antonio must pay out his contract with his life:

> I have engaged myself to a dear friend,
> Engaged my friend to his mere enemy,
> To feed my means. Here is a letter, lady,
> The paper as the body of my friend,
> And every word in it a gaping wound
> Issuing life-blood.
>
> (3.2.259–64)

Each phrase here twists like a knife, true to a play-world in which words are wounds and paper a body that bleeds to death.

It is no wonder that the advertisement on the title page of the play's first edition says what it does:

> With the extreame crueltie of *Shylocke* the Jewe towards the sayd Merchant, in cutting a just pound of his fleshe and the obtayning of *Portia* by the choyce of three chests.

The Quarto here advertises two of the play's great attractions – clearly popular scenes when it was played by the Lord Chamberlain's Men. But it tells us perhaps more than was intended. First, it claims that Shylock actually cuts the pound of flesh from Antonio. Second, it seems to identify this cruelty with the obtaining of Portia in the casket scene. Both interpretations, we might justly say, are wrong. Shylock intends the cut, but is foiled; the choice of caskets has nothing to do with 'extreame crueltie'. But both are also in a sense right. In the world of the casket scene, fairness is foul, life breeds from the tomb, and love is defined as sacrifice and torture.

Even the most rarefied, sophisticated comedies cannot escape death. Consider *Love's Labour's Lost*. It has a reputation as a play besotted with words, a dazzlingly pointless combat of wits. But consider the play's first words, as the King of Navarre explains why he intends to spend three years in academic isolation with his mates, hidden away from all public and erotic congress:

> Let fame, that all hunt after in their lives,
> Live registered upon our brazen tombs,
> And then grace us in the disgrace of death
> When, spite of cormorant devouring time,
> Th'endeavour of this present breath may buy
> That honour which shall bate his scythe's keen edge
> And make us heirs of all eternity.
>
> (1.1.1–7)

It seems for a moment as though the King is spurning the vain pursuit of 'fame', leaving it for the lottery of death and posthumous reputation. But no. Whatever he is about to declare, whatever his band of brothers is about to undertake ('th'endeavour of this present breath'), it will be a direct *taking on* of death – not only nullifying its destructiveness ('bate his scythe's keen edge'), but also scripting its content, turning 'disgrace' into 'grace' and making his little coterie 'heirs of all eternity'. There is more here than a longing for fame beyond death. The King's ambition is much greater, much more spiritually and temporally presumptuous. He is arrogating to himself the most enormous power of redemption: an overcoming of death.

The King's spiritual liberty-taking is in some ways typical of a comic take on death. It turns away from death, as though something hideously beyond the pale. Equally, it tries to outdo death, not so much by leaping beyond it as by turning death into a condition that can be survived, even triumphed over. His academy is death without sting, a baroque pseudo-imitation of the 'brazen tomb': a delightful mix of seclusion (like the grave) and glory (because they are saved).

But his ambition is also a kind of false comedy. He wants to set up his court as a 'little academe, / Still and contemplative in living art' (1.1.13–14). Notice the oxymorons (unintended by the King): 'still' and 'living'; living only as 'art'. As the action quickly reveals, to stay in this hermetic, self-pleased privacy, warring against affections, fighting desires, is to be effectively entombed. This is why the aristocrats' pretensions must be so quickly exposed, as their resolve collapses the moment they behold an actual woman.

The King's existential evasiveness and redemptive pretensions – his fraudulent pre-empting of death – are symptomatic of a wider bad faith that Shakespeare ascribes to a particular kind of boastful, inflated, applause-seeking wit. This comes home to roost in the play's notorious refusal to end happily. Just as we might be expecting the various suitors to pair off with their lovers, a messenger, one Monsieur Mercadé, arrives for the Princess:

> *Mercadé*   I am sorry, madam, for the news I bring
> Is heavy in my tongue. The King, your father –

Figure 23 Disection of human cadavers had been prohibited in England before the sixteenth century. It was only in Shakespeare's lifetime that dissection for the study of anatomy was permitted for the fellows of the Royal College of Physicians. Andreas Vesalius's seminal study of the human body, *De humani corporis fabrica*, was printed in Basle in 1543. On the title page, death holds a fool's ribbons on a staff. Bodleian Library, B 1.16 Med., title page.

ANDREAE VESALII
BRVXELLENSIS, SCHOLAE
medicorum Patauinæ profeſſoris, de
Humani corporis fabrica
Libri ſeptem.

CVM CAESAREAE
Maieſt. Galliarum Regis, ac Senatus Veneti gra-
tia & priuilegio, ut in diplomatis eorundem continetur.

Figure 24 Holinshed's witches are not the hags of later stage tradition or of Elizabethan witchcraft trials, but rather 'nymphs or fairies' with an unsettlingly direct understanding of mortality. *The Chronicles of England, Scotlande, and Irelande*, by Raphael Holinshed, 1577. Bodleian Library, Douce H 240.

| *Princess* | Dead, for my life. |
| *Mercadé* | Even so; my tale is told. |

(5.2.711–13)

That the Princess anticipates the news suggests guilty forgetfulness, as though aware of the home truth neglected amid all the nonsense. But the King admits no such remembrance, and proceeds with verbose conceitedness to deny the claims of the reaper:

> And though the mourning brow of progeny
> Forbid the smiling courtesy of love
> The holy suit which fain it would convince,
> Yet since love's argument was first on foot,
> Let not the cloud of sorrow jostle it
> From what it purposed, since to wail friends lost
> Is not by much so wholesome-profitable
> As to rejoice at friends but newly found.

(736–43)

The inanity of his plea is typified in its contradictory approach to time and succession – or, in other words, to the present fact of death's dire interruption. First he says that the Princess's grief as a daughter ('the mourning brow of progeny') must give way because 'love's argument was first on foot' – a statement both factually wrong (she was her father's child before she was his intended bride) and emotionally obtuse. Then he declares that 'lost' friends should give way to friends 'newly found', the logic being that wailing is less profitable than rejoicing. It is no wonder that the Princess's reply is so curt and tart: 'I understand you not' (744). The joke in this response is mainly against the King's pseudo-courtly obscurity. But the obscurity is the servant of a prior existential falseness, one that pretends we really can write our own scripts, establish our own rules, screen off both past and future in the interests of protecting an ever-new, ever-flattering present.

The King is scripted as a hothouse imbecile – a figure with no more depth than a playing card, aware of nothing beyond the game he thinks he is in, a figure of the purest existential shallowness. And it is death that exposes him and his false consciousness. Death is the enemy of thin, facile comedy.

Conversely, death is the necessary abettor of any comedy that will grip, touch and endure. True comedy, Shakespeare seems to be saying, can only prosper in the wake and in the imminence of death. This explains the fierce challenge that the mysterious dark-eyed Rosaline sets the glibly irreverent semi-hero Biron:

> You shall this twelvemonth term from day to day
> Visit the speechless sick and still converse
> With groaning wretches, and your task shall be
> With all the fierce endeavour of your wit
> To enforce the painèd impotent to smile.
>
> (5.2.836–40)

Biron is horrified by the sentence:

> To move wild laughter in the throat of death? –
> It cannot be, it is impossible.
>
> (841–2)

Rosaline's aim is to 'choke' him of his 'gibing spirit' and 'idle scorns', an aim in which death will be her partner, staring down at the jesting man, daring him to keep on prattling. To the extent that this prescription refers to Shakespeare's own practice, it is saying farewell to a comedy of repartee and superior parody and self-pleasing cleverness. And indeed Shakespeare never again writes a play that can be characterized in this way. Instead he writes particular characters who display, suffer or are cured of the compulsively witty malady – for example, Benedick in *Much Ado*, Mercutio in *Romeo and Juliet*, Falstaff in *Henry IV*. In each case a pathological devotion to joking seems premised on a denial of depth, love and death: Benedick running away from memory until overhearing his own lies; Falstaff haunted by the death he knows is coming; Mercutio possessed by life-denying jokes that will eventually come true, and end him. These examples in turn suggest another interpretation of Rosaline's challenge and Biron's response. That is, Shakespeare himself will endeavour to 'move wild laughter *in the throat of death*' – not simply make the sick laugh, or have death as an imaginary audience, briefly appeased by the entertainment. The deeper meaning is that the 'throat of death' itself should be entered, and move, and speak its 'wild laughter'. This laughter is no contented chuckle; it isn't the unanimity of an audience, happy to be entertained. Far from the cosy monument of praise envisaged by the King in his first speech, death becomes a kind of wilderness, beyond custom, beyond decorum, beyond domestic or courtly possession. And so too will be its expression. Death will not be ceremoniously marked or honoured, as in public rituals of remembrance. It will be felt, feared, and even endured. This is the rage, the terror, the despair that we hear in the excesses of a Falstaff or a Mercutio; it is the bass note of Hamlet, in the cruelty and suffering of his wit; it is the mirthless cackle of Macbeth's witches, speaking always from the netherlands, where they have seen and known too much.

Vssi affin que le ciel etheré
Ne fust desoy plusque terre asseuré
Les fiers geans cõme on dit affecterõt

4

A Plague on Your Houses

Shakespeare's life was bracketed by the plague. Three months after the record of his baptism in April 1564 in the register of Holy Trinity Church, Stratford upon Avon, came the ominous inscription: *Hic incepit pestis* (Here begins the plague). The baby did well to avoid the contagion, and to survive a mortality rate in Stratford that year that was four times that of the previous plague-free year. In *A Room of One's Own*, Virginia Woolf famously imagined 'Shakespeare's sister', Judith, as an exemplary figure embodying the historical and continuing difficulties for the woman writer: Shakespeare's actual older sisters Joan and Margaret both died in infancy before he was born. Getting through childhood was touch and go for Elizabethan children. (It was even more dangerous in Shakespeare's plays, where the infant mortality rate is almost 100 per cent: think of the princes in *Richard III*, young prince Arthur in *King John*, the Macduffs' 'fry' in *Macbeth*, *The Winter's Tale*'s Mamillius.)

This childhood escape seems, in retrospect, to symbolize the ongoing place of the plague in Shakespeare's imagination. It is everywhere – but ultimately harmless. The plague is rhetorically ubiquitous in phrases such as Falstaff's unconvincing bragging 'A plague of all cowards!' (*1 Henry IV*, 2.5.117) or Troilus' exclamation 'O gods, how do you plague me!' (*Troilus and Cressida*, 1.1.94) but literally virtually absent. Men and women die in Shakespeare's plays in any number of inventive ways. In *Othello* Desdemona is smothered in her bed; in *Titus Andronicus* the rapist Goths Chiron and Demetrius have their throats cut and are baked in pastry; John of Gaunt dies of old age, exacerbated by the absence of his

Figure 25 This French translation of one of Shakespeare's preferred sources, Ovid's *Metamorphoses*, shows the same spectacular violence expressed in *Titus Andronicus*: the eating of human flesh. Bodleian Library, MS. Douce 117, 13v.

exiled son Bolingbroke in *Richard II*; in *Hamlet* Ophelia drowns, as the gravedigger reflects, either because she went to the water or because the water came to her. But no one in Shakespeare's plays dies of the plague. Just as Shakespeare never sets a play in contemporary London, neither does he address directly the most prominent cause of sudden mortality in his society. Contemporary or documentary realism is, after all, not Shakespeare's style. It is to other literary forms and authors – in particular Thomas Dekker, who wrote a series of feverishly inventive, sardonic prose pamphlets on the plague – that we must look to find the effects of plague on early modern society.

Thomas Lodge identified the full and devastating range of plague pathology:

> Alienation, and frenzy, blueness and blackness appearing about the sores and carbuncles, and after their appearances the sudden vanishings of the same, cold in the extreme parts, and intolerable heat in the inward, unquenchable thirst, continually soundings, urines white, and crude, or red, troubled and black: Cold sweat about the forehead and face; cramps, blackness in the excrements of the body, stench, and blueness, the flux of the belly, with weakness of the heart, shortness of breath, and great stench of the same, lack of sleep, and appetite to eat, profound sleep, changing of colour in the face, exchanged to paleness, blackness, or blueness, cogitation or great unquietness.[7]

Here is a range of somatic symptoms with which Londoners must have been neurotically familiar. Outbreaks of plague in 1592, in 1603–4 and in 1606 punctuated and shaped London life and Shakespeare's writing career. The death toll for the 1603 outbreak, the year too of Elizabeth's death, as marked by Dekker in his sardonically titled pamphlet *The Wonderful Year*, is estimated at about one in five of the London population.[8] Broadsides of 1636 and 1637 (Figures 2 and 26) beg forgiveness for the city, recording these earlier periods of pestilence and the mortality figures. An illustration (Figure 2) shows bodies awaiting burial as citizens fleeing the infected city, in the upper left of the woodcut, are greeted by villagers armed with pitchforks desperate to keep plague from their own doors. When plague struck, mortality rates were around 60 per cent or higher. The terrors of the plague are a paradox in Shakespeare's work: omnipresent but obscured.

Figure 26 This review of recent plague epidemics published in 1637 combines historical record of mortality numbers with a woodcut showing a skeleton Death embracing the walled city, and a prayer acknowledging 'we must dye all'. Bodleian Library, Wood 416 (3).

LONDONS
LORD HAVE MERCY VPON VS.

A true Relation of five modern *Plagues* or *Visitations* in *London*, with the number of all the Diseased that were buried:
viz: The first in the yeare of Queen *Elizabeth*, *Anno* 1592, the second in the yeare 1603, the third in that (never to be forgotten yeare) 1625.
The fourth in *Anno* 1630. The fift this now present *Visitation* 1636, which the LORD of his mercy deliver *London* and *England* from.

Certain approved Medicines for the Plague, both to prevent that contagion, and to expell after it be taken, as have been approved in Anno 1625. as also in this present Visitation 1636.

A cheape Medicine to keepe from infection.

TAke a pinte of new milke, and cut two cloves of Garlicke very small, put it in the milke, and drinke it mornings fasting, and it preserveth from infection.

READER, what ever thou art, rich or poore,
Rowse up thy selfe, for death stands at the
If God sayes strike, he must & wil come in (dore;
For death we know is the reward of sinne.
His very breath is so infectious growne,
He poysons every one he breathes upon;
He is the rich mans terrour, makes him flye,
And beare away his bagges, as loath to dye.
What shall the poore doe that behind do stay?
Death makes them rich by taking them away.
But what shall poore men do, then that doe live,
Tis surely fit the rich should comfort give,
And weekely meanes unto them still afford,
When his rich purse he knows can wel afford.
Doth make them fearefull of that punishment
Due unto sinne, for time that's evill spent.
Oh why was this not thought on long agoe!
When God expected our repentance fo?
When fixe yeares since, a little Plague God sent,
He shoke his rod to move us to repent:
Not long before that time, a dearth of corne
Was sent to us to see if we would turne:
And the last Summer none deny it can,
The beasts did suffer for the sinne of man:
Grasse was so short and small, that it was told,
Hey for foure pound a load was daily sold.
These judgements God hath sent even to cite us
Unto repentance, and from sinne to fright us.
Oh stubborne *England*! childish and unwise,
So heavy laden with iniquities.

Returne, returne, unto thy loving Father,
Returne I say, and so much the rather,
Because his Sonne thy Saviour pleads thy cause,
Though thou hast broken all his holy lawes:
Say to thy selfe, my sinnes are cause of all
Gods judgements that upon this land doth fall,
And sin's the cause that each one doth complain
They have too much, sometimes too little raine:
Say to thy selfe, this Plague may be removed,
If I repent, as plainly may be proved
By *Niniveh*, that Citie great and large,
For God hath given to his Angels charge,
To strike and to forbeare as he sees fit;
Let all infected houses be thy Text,
And make this use, that thine may be the next.
The red crosse still is us'd, as it hath bin,
To shew they Christians are that are within.
And Lord have mercy on us on the dore,
Puts thee in minde to pray for them therefore.
The watchman that attends the house of sorrow,
He may attend upon thy house to morrow.
Oh where's the vows we to our God have made!
When death & sicknesse came with axe & spade,
And hurld our brethren up in heaps apace,
Even forty thousand in a little space:
And now againe he doth with us begin,
T'increase the Plague, as we increase in sinne:
Each spectacle of death and funerall,
Puts thee and I in minde we must dye all.

A Prayer fit to be used in this time of sicknesse and mortality.

O Lord God, strong and mighty, great and fearefull, which dwellest in the heavens, and workest great wonders; we thy miserable children here on earth, doe most humbly beseech thee to be mercifull unto us, to pardon our English offences, and forgive us all our sinnes: O Lord enter not into judgement with thy servants, for if thou doe, there shall no flesh be saved in thy sight: we confesse and acknowledge O Lord, that it is our sinnes which have moved thee to wrath, and to shew such fearefull tokens of thy displeasure towards us in these our dayes; first by locking up the heavens that no raine should fall to succour the earth, neverthelesse upon our repentance and humility, it hath pleased thee of thy fatherly goodnesse to send downe some sweet comfortable showers of thy mercy upon the earth. O Lord increase our thankfulnesse, and give us grace to amend our lives, that thou maist turne from us all those judgements which we most righteously have deserved; thou hast sent thy messengers of mercy, thy Ministers of thy holy Word to allure us by faire meanes to repentance, thou hast sent Monsters from the Sea, and cast them upon our English shore, fearefull and strange to behold, to cry out against us; nay, thou hast suffered the tempter, that old enemy of mans salvation, to worke upon the weakenesse of some of our poore brethren, to assume unto themselves the names of Prophets, to prophecie evill against this nation; but thou hast disclosed the subtilty of the Serpent unto us, that as he was a lyer from the beginning, so thou hast proved his Prophets to be false Prophets, by sending downe these sweet and comfortable showers of raine upon the earth, giving us to understand, that Prophecying is ceast, and that no man is worthy to know the secrets of thy will. Neverthelesse though we are not Prophets, nor Prophets children, yet wee cannot but expect utter desolation and destruction without speedy repentance: Give us, O give us repentant hearts, that we may be truely humbled at the sight of our sinnes, and walke in newnesse of life all the dayes of our life: wee beseech thee good Father to turne in mercy to us, and remove from us this Sicknesse lately begun among us: LORD command the destroying Angell to hold his hand, that our brethren which are fled from us for the preservation of their lives, may returne againe with ioy, that we with them may praise and glorifie thy name, now and for evermore, Amen.

Written by H. C.

LONDON Printed for *Richard Harper*, at the Hospitall Gate in Smithfield.

Left column table (1603)

An exact and true relation of the number of those that died in London and the Liberties of all diseases, from the 17 of March 1602, to the 22. of December, 1603.

	totall.	Pl.
March 17	108	3
March 24	60	2
March 31	78	6
Aprill 7	66	4
Aprill 14	79	4
Aprill 28	98	8
May 5	199	10
May 12	122	18
May 19	122	22
May 26	122	32
June 2	114	30
June 9	131	43
June 16	144	59
June 23	182	72
June 30	267	158
July 7	445	263
July 14	612	424

The Out-parishes this weeke were joyned with the Citie.

	totall.	Pl.
July 21	1186	917
July 28	1728	1395
August 4	2256	1925
August 11	2077	1742
August 18	3054	2719
August 25	2853	2539
Septemb.1	3385	3024
Septemb.8	3078	2728
Septem.15	3129	2815
Septem.22	2456	2195
Septem.29	1961	1732
Octob. 6	1831	1649
Octob. 13	1312	1142
Octob. 20		
Nov. 3	763	625
Decem. 1	223	105
Decem. 8	163	55
Decem.15	200	66
Decem.22	168	74

The totall of the Burials this whole Yeare, 38250. Of the Plague 30583.

1625.

Buried in London and the Liberties, of all Diseases, Anno 1625. the number here following.

	totall.	Pl.
March 17	261	4
March 24	216	8
March 31	243	11
Aprill 7	239	10
Aprill 14	256	24
Aprill 21	230	25
Aprill 28	305	26
May 5	292	30
May 12	332	45
May 19	379	71
May 26	401	78
June 2	395	69
June 9	434	91
June 16	510	165
June 23	640	239
June 30	942	390
July 7	1222	593
July 14	1781	1004
July 21	2850	1819
July 28	3583	2471
August 4	4517	3659
August 11	4855	4115
August 18	5205	4463
August 25	4841	4218
Septemb.1	3897	3344
Septemb.8	3157	2550
Septem.15	2148	1672
Septem.22	1994	1551
Septem.29	1236	852
Octob. 6	833	538
Octob. 13	815	511
Octob. 20	651	331
Octob. 27	375	134
Nov. 3	357	89
Nov. 10	319	92
Nov. 17	274	48
Nov. 24	321	27
Decem. 1	290	15
Decem. 8	185	9
Decem.15	168	6
Decem.22	157	3

The totall of the Burials this Yeare, 54018. Of the Plague 35403.

1592.

	totall.	Pl.
March 17	351	31
March 24	219	29
March 31	307	17
Aprill 7	203	33
Aprill 14	290	37
Aprill 21	330	41
May 5	350	29
May 12	339	38
May 19	450	43
May 26	410	62
June 2	441	81
June 9	399	99
June 16	401	108
June 23	850	118
June 30	1440	227
July 7	1512	893
July 14	1491	255
July 21	1507	852
July 28	1503	983
August 4	1550	797
August 11	1532	651
August 18	1508	449
August 25	2490	507
Septemb.1	1210	563
Septemb.15	629	349
Septem.22	450	139
Septem.29	408	130
Octob. 6	422	223
Octob. 13	330	208
Octob. 20	320	301
Octob. 27	310	271
Novem. 3	309	209
Nov. 10	301	107
Nov. 17	321	91
Decemb. 1	331	86
Decem. 8	329	71
Decem. 16	386	39

	totall.	Pl.
June 24	105	19
July 1	109	43
July 8	113	41
July 15	150	50
July 22	139	49
July 29	179	77
August 5	150	56
August 12	146	65
August 19	269	54
August 26	170	67
Septem. 2	120	60
Septem. 9	259	63
Septem.15	264	68
Septem.23	274	57
Septem.29	169	56
Octob. 14	261	73
Octob. 21	108	48
Octob. 28	214	34
Novem. 4	243	39
Nov. 11	215	49
Nov. 18	200	18
Nov. 25	126	7
Decem. 2	198	19
Decem. 16	117	5

The totall of all the buriall this yeare, is of all diseases 10554. Of the Plague 1317.

1636

Buried in London and the liberties, of all diseases, the number as followeth.

	totall.	Pl.
Aprill 7	199	4
Aprill 14	205	5

This weeke was added the City Parishes.

S. Marg. Westminster.
Lambeth.
S. Mary Newington.
Redrife Parish.
S. Mary Islington.
Stepney Parish.
Hackney Parish.

	totall.	Pl.
April 21	285	14
April 28	259	27
May 5	251	19
May 12	308	55
May 19	299	63
May 26	330	62
June 2	339	67
June 9	345	87
June 16	381	103
June 23	304	73
June 30	353	104
July 7	115	83
July 14	372	104
July 21	395	120
July 28	423	151
August 4	461	206
August 11	538	283
August 18	638	321
August 25	787	419
Septemb.1	1159	650
Septemb.8	1669	650
Septem.15	1206	867
Septem.22	1125	865
Novem.3	1109	1109
Novem.10	1104	715
Nov. 17	850	173
Nov. 24	817	476
Decem. 1	614	353
Decem. 8	419	437
Decem. 15	385	65
Decem. 22	316	76
Decem. 29	383	125

The totall of the Burials this yeare 17415. Of the Plague 12102.

1637.

Buried in London and the liberties, of all diseases, the number as followeth.

	totall.	Pl.
January 5	381	126
January 12	314	73
January 19	268	59
January 26	289	72
Februar. 2	351	103
Februar. 9	315	104
Februar. 16	285	85
Februar. 23	324	44
March 2	261	69
March 9	332	100
March 16	303	80
March 23	311	86
March 31	343	115
April 7	301	98
April 14	282	79
April 21	300	90
April 28	339	107
May 5	292	81
May 12	320	105

Newcastle / Gateshead table

	Buried of all diseases in Newcastle, as followeth.		Buried in Gateshead in Newcastle as followeth.	
	totall	Pl.	totall	Pl.
May 21	59		May 30	19
June 28	55		June 6	24
June 11	111		June 14	40
June 18	99		June 20	54
June 25	162		July 4	75
July 2	133		July 11	55
July 9	172		July 16	60
July 16	184		August 1	39
July 23	149		August 8	18
July 30	270		August 15	23
Aug. 12	334		August 21	33
Aug. 20	402		August 29	38
Septem. 3	430		Septem. 5	37
Septem.17	460		Septem. 12	17
Septem.10	290		Septem. 19	14
Septem.24	136		Septem. 26	6
Octob. 1	80		Octob. 2	1
Octob. 15	63		Octob. 9	4

The totall is 4764. The totall is 545.

One thing is certain: the plague outbreak in London of 1592 did nothing to halt Shakespeare's fledgling career as a writer. The closure of the theatres as a precaution when plague deaths in London rose above thirty a week meant that he needed to diversify. Under these apparently unpropitious circumstances Shakespeare wrote his best-selling work *Venus and Adonis*, published in 1593. Its signed dedication to Henry Wriothesley, the Earl of Southampton, is the first appearance of Shakespeare's name in print. Like its darker sibling *The Rape of Lucrece*, also dedicated to Southampton and published the following year, this poem turns on female agency (unlike most of the drama of the period). Both poems record the oblique pressure of plague, in details of their language and imagery, and in their narrative telos: and they register a possible alternative future for the young writer as a poet under aristocratic patronage rather than a dramatist for the public theatres.

Venus and Adonis tells the story of the goddess's desire for a beautiful young boy who prefers hunting to sex. It develops a short episode in Ovid's *Metamorphoses* into a poem of almost 1,200 lines, part of the fashionable contemporary genre known as epyllia, or mini-epic, in which Christopher Marlowe and John Marston also published at this time. Epyllia were classical soft-porn poems aimed at young men in the London Inns of Court. We might see their intensely erotic teleology as a kind of *carpe diem* motif encouraged by the context of plague deaths, particularly since the epidemiology of the plague suggests that young people in their teens and twenties were most susceptible to its ravages. Venus apostrophizes her unwilling young lover's lips in terms that cannot suppress the urgency of the plague year.

Figures 27 and 28 Two editions of Shakespeare's most popular work in print, *Venus and Adonis*. Both copies have interesting provenance: the first, published in 1593, is the only known surviving copy of the first edition previously owned by Frances Wolfreston, one of the earliest attested female readers of Shakespeare. The second, published in 1602, was given to the library by Robert Burton, author of *The Anatomy of Melancholy*, who has written his name on the title page. Bodleian Library Arch. G e.31 (2) and Arch. G f.3 (2).

'Long may they kiss each other, for this cure!
O, never let their crimson liveries wear,
And as they last, their verdure still endure,
To drive infection from the dangerous year,
  That the star-gazers, having writ on death,
  May say the plague is banished by thy breath!'

(505–10)

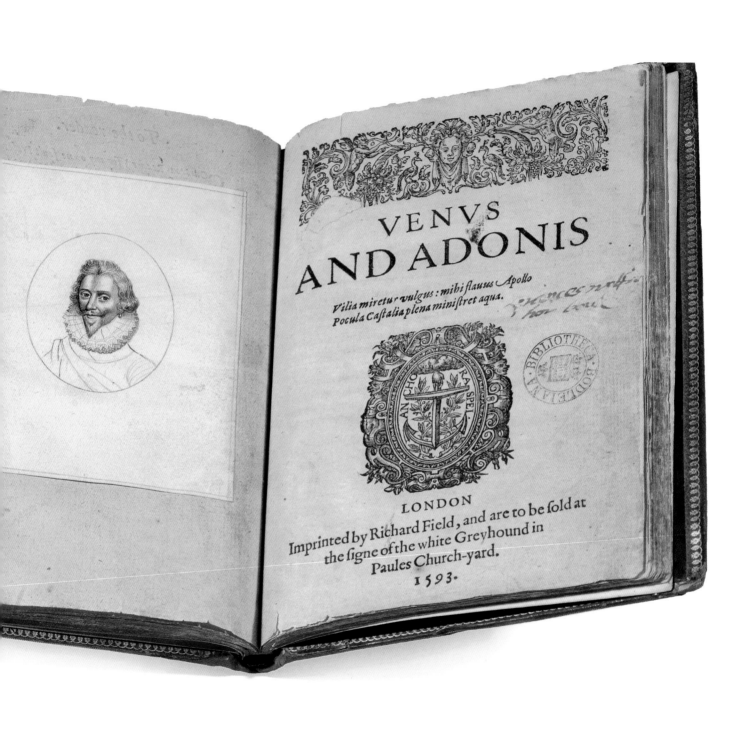

VENVS
AND ADONIS

Vilia miretur vulgus: mihi flauus Apollo
Pocula Castalia plena ministret aqua.

LONDON

Imprinted by Richard Field, and are to be sold at
the signe of the white Greyhound in
Paules Church-yard.
1593.

VENUS
AND ADONIS.

Vilia miretur vulgus : mihi flauus Apollo
Pocula Caſtalia plena miniſtret aqua.

Imprinted at London for *William Leake,*
dwelling at the ſigne of the Holy Ghoſt, in
Pauls Churchyard. 1602.

3

The posies of sweet-smelling herbs and flowers carried as a prophylactic from the plague – memorialized in the children's rhyme deriving from the plague 'Ring a ring o' roses' – are the crimson and verdure of Adonis's protective sweet breath. Venus tries to persuade her unwilling swain that 'fruitless chastity' 'on the earth would breed a scarcity / And barren dearth of daughters and of sons', calling his virginal body 'a swallowing grave' (751–4). Adonis, by contrast, figures her love as 'sweating lust' 'blotting' his 'fresh beauty' rather like the plague (794–6). The fear of death and the allure of sexual attraction are elided in a poem that is steeped in the atmosphere of contemporary London even as it attempts to escape to a classical arcadia.

Venus and Adonis sets up the narrative situation that Shakespeare's later career as playwright attunes us to see as comic – in particular, a woman's active desire for an apparently younger or less worldly-wise lover, as in the relationship between Rosalind and Orlando in *As You Like It*, or, more darkly, between Helen and Bertram in *All's Well That Ends Well*. These romantic comedy plots are heading towards marriage and, implicitly, the renewal of human society exemplified in the crowded celebratory stages of their final scenes.

But although *Venus and Adonis* follows this narrative shape in certain ways, its outcome is darker. Venus's unrequited desire is not life-affirming but ultimately fatal. Adonis is pierced by the tusk of a boar, but that Venus is really the phallic threat to the young man is made clear in her admission: 'Had I been toothed like [the boar], I must confess / With kissing him I should have killed him first' (1117–18). And Adonis's transfiguration in death into a 'purple flower … chequered with white' (1168) may well be the first literary reference to the snakeshead fritillary, but it also poeticizes and repurposes the blotched skin of the plague victim as the beautiful pigmentation of the flower. Venus 'hies' away in her chariot to her own plagued quarantine: the poem's final lines tell us that the amorous 'queen / Means to immure herself, and not be seen' (1193–4).

Plague-consciousness also seeps into the language of Shakespeare's other early narrative poem, *The Rape of Lucrece*. Threatened by Tarquin, Lucrece bewails 'opportunity', by which 'The patient dies while the physician sleeps' and 'Advice is sporting while infection breeds' (903–6). The sense that the plague is waiting in the wings is palpable. It works poetically as a metaphor for the threat of Tarquin's lust, but in articulating a real contemporary fear the metaphor exceeds its subservient syntax to become the real unspeakable threat of the poem. Again, Dekker's plague writing amplifies the implicit association. In *The Wonderful Year* he observes 'beautiful maidens thrown on their beds and ravished by sickness', including a hapless bride: 'Death rudely lay with her and spoiled her of a maidenhead in spite of her husband.'[9] Lucrece's inability to persuade Tarquin from her rape despite her piteous eloquence humanizes the impossibility of negotiating with plague, even as moralists exhorted prayer and godly living as a prophylactic.

Burning sexual desire can thus be interpreted as a response to living under the shadow of plague, as well as a metaphor for its sudden, physically experienced onset. Venus draws on this pestilential context:

> 'As burning fevers, agues pale and faint,
> Life-poisoning pestilence, and frenzies wood,
> The marrow-eating sickness, whose attaint
> Disorder breeds by heating of the blood;
>   Surfeits, impostumes, grief, and damned despair
>   Swear nature's death for framing thee so fair.'
>
>   (*Venus and Adonis* 739–44)

Plague's symptoms of sudden fever, racing pulse and pains could be aligned with – and perhaps thereby robbed of some of their existential terrors – the groans and dolours of unrequited love. As the comic servant Speed puts it in *The Two Gentlemen of Verona* among a catalogue of 'special marks' of the lover, 'to walk alone, like one that had the pestilence' is a sure sign of being 'in love' (2.1.17, 20, 72). Beatrice uses the same imagery scornfully of Benedick in the opening scene of *Much Ado About Nothing*: 'He is sooner caught than the pestilence, and the taker runs presently mad' (1.1.82–3). *Twelfth Night* allies it again with the unsought and devastating onset of love. 'How now?' muses Olivia, mourning her dead brother but newly invigorated by her encounter with the enigmatic messenger Cesario:

> Even so quickly may one catch the plague?
> Methinks I feel this youth's perfections
> With an invisible and subtle stealth
> To creep in at mine eyes.
>
> (1.5.284–8)

She echoes, unknowingly, Orsino's praise from the beginning of the play: 'Methought she purged the air of pestilence' (1.1.19).

Plague here is associated not with death and destruction, but with physiological changes that are extreme but pleasurable. Olivia's elision of plague infection with watching also allies it with the experience of theatre. Theatres were closed as a response to plague for a complicated set of overlapping reasons. Since the causes of infection and its transmission were imperfectly understood, the theatres were seen as both physiological and moral breeding grounds. Writing to the Privy Council in 1600 to try to restrict the number of playhouses in the city, the Aldermen of London identified the transmission of disease as one of their complaints:

> In the time of sickness it is found by experience that many, having sores and yet not heartsick, take occasion hereby to walk abroad and to recreate themselves by hearing a play. Whereby others are infect, and themselves also many things miscarry.[10]

Anti-theatrical writers developed the correlation between theatre and plague into causation, arguing that it was not simply that a large crowd gathered and thereby spread infection, but that the very act of theatre was itself a kind of moral contagion.

Plague, like theatre, was an urban phenomenon which attacked the body politic. As Steven Mullaney has it in his study of the early modern London suburbs, theatre was 'a plague in its own right, contaminating morals and manners

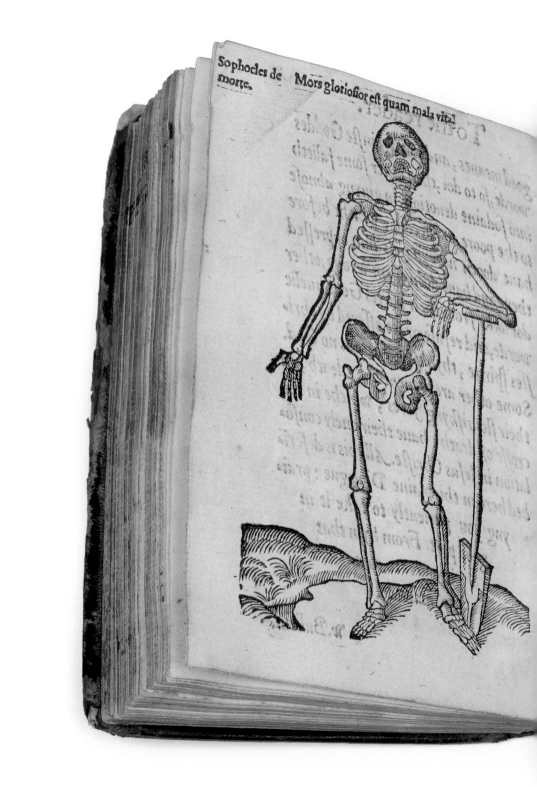

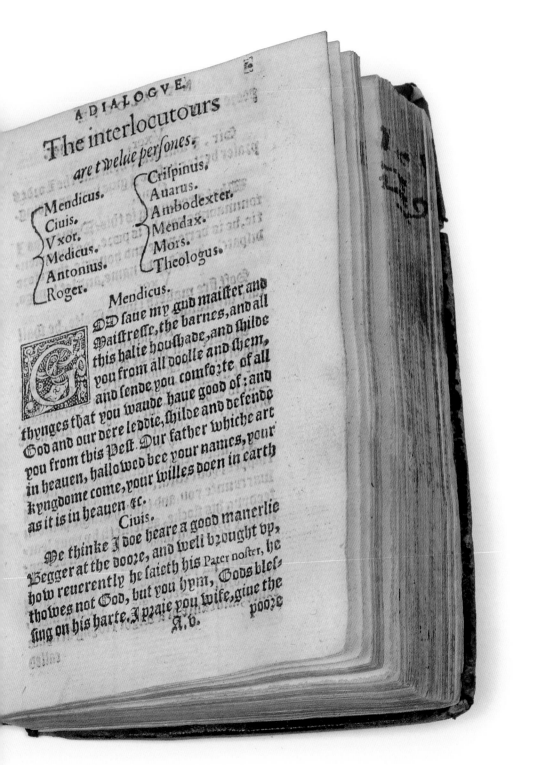

A DIALOGVE.

The interlocutours
are twelue persones.

{ Mendicus.
Ciuis.
Vxor.
Medicus.
Antonius.
Roger.

{ Crispinus.
Auarus.
Ambodexter.
Mendax.
Mors.
Theologus.

Mendicus.

GOD saue my gud maister and Maistresse, the barnes, and all this halie houshade, and shilde you from all doolle and shem, and sende you comforte of all thynges that you waude haue good of: and God and our dere leddie, shilde and defende you from this Pest. Our father whiche art in heauen, hallowed bee your names, your kyngdome come, your willes doen in earth as it is in heauen. &c.

Ciuis.

Me thinke I doe heare a good manerlie Begger at the doore, and well brought vp, how reuerently he saieth his Pater noster, he thowes not God, but you hym, Gods blessing on his harte. I praie you wife, giue the poore

A.b.

Figure 29 William Bullein's dialogue on the plague combined wit, satire, and moral tales in a pamphlet that slyly connected physical and political pestilence. *A dialogue bothe pleasaunte and pietifull, wherein is a goodly regimente against the fever pestilence with a consolacion and comfort against death* by William Bullein, 1573. Bodleian Library, 8° E 9(2) Med. Sig. A4v.

when it did not, in its pathological alliance, contaminate the flesh itself'.[11] The Puritan controversialist William Prynne wrote in the seventeenth century that 'The Playhaunters are contagious in quality, more apt to poison, to infect all those who dare approach them, than one who is full of plague-sores.'[12] Dekker personified plague Death not in the common iconography of the skeleton in the European Dance of Death or *danse macabre* tradition, but with an image much closer to the play-world of the Elizabethan theatre: 'Death ... like a stalking Tamburlaine hath pitched his tents ... in the sinful suburbs'[13] – the suburbs were the place of the theatre, where Christopher Marlowe's ruthless Scythian conqueror Tamburlaine held his military court. In the early modern imagination, theatre and plague were the closest of conceptual cousins.

Plague gets a mention in just about every one of Shakespeare's works. Caliban curses his imperial overlord:

You taught me language, and my profit on't
Is I know how to curse. The red plague rid you
For learning me your language!

(*The Tempest*, 1.2.365–7).

Henry V predicts that the putrefaction of French dead on the battlefield 'shall breed a plague' (*Henry V*, 4.3.104). Crossed by his daughter Goneril, Lear calls her a 'plague-sore' (*King Lear*, 2.2.397), and later he bids plagues 'light on my daughters' (3.4.64). John of Gaunt's famous eulogy to England idealizes 'this sceptered isle' a 'fortress built by nature for herself / Against infection' (*Richard II*, 2.1.40, 43–4).

In *Romeo and Juliet* – one of Shakespeare's earliest tragedies – individual tragedy is offset by plague's indiscriminate ravages. The play is marked from the outset by the inevitability of death. The Prologue describes the young couple's 'death-marked love' (Chorus 9), and Romeo in particular is haunted by foreboding. These fateful harbingers are fulfilled in the play's decisive action – its central point of no return – the death of Mercutio. Killed accidentally after Romeo intervenes

Figure 30 Death here is a ballad musician, reminding the hearers of recent appearances including at the Oxfordshire Assizes (for the hanging of convicts), and inviting the audience to dance with him to heaven. Bodleian Library, Wood 401 (60) (c. 1625).

The dolefull Dance and Song of Death; Intituled,
Dance after my Pipe,
To a pleasant new tune.

(left column, partly cut off:)

```
oœn dainty: and part.
with his own rod;
e fall of Folly,

on her knœ,
r age with store,
did agrœ
had made before.
œp alone:
 fostered child,
ve upon,
 the world so wilde.
 company
uths of Mars his train,
 jeopardy,
ur for my pain:
eged walls
ing, rain and snow,
 with powred Balls,
arks are yet to show.
ored tok their rest
 a stately Bed,
pavement was my nest
low for my head:
h as I could get,
rbs of sundry sorts,
nt my hungry mind,
ommons were but short.
 to salt my meat,
 a gilded Cup,
ink as I could get,
Ditch I drank it up:
apes by my side,
arg'd with match & light,
onth I did abide
 and watch by night.
orious bain,
 grew stiffe and lame,
me home again,
 such costly same:
home I made a proof
ould do if nœd should be,
esfolks lokt aloof,
y had forgotten me.
l by chattering charms
 of other Birds,
oondring at my harms,
 no relief but words:
nt while they have store,
equall every way,
e lent them somwhat mor
en as good as they.
Death and end my grief,
ds ring forth my knell,
breast be the chief
nd so farewell.
ouldier be dismaid
eld with courage bold,
words that I have said,
friends when thou art old.
```

Can you dance the shaking of the Shéets,
  a Dance that every one must do,
Can you trim it up with dainty swéets,
  and every thing that 'longs thereto?
Make ready then your winding shéet,
And sée how pée can bestir your féet,
  For Death is the man that all must mée.

Bring away the Begger and the King,
  and every man in his degrée,
Bring away the old and youngest thing,
  come all to Death and follow me:
The Courtier with his lofty loks,
The Lawyer with his learned Boks,
The Banker with his baiting hoks.

Merchants, have you made your Part in
  in Italy, and all about?   (France.
Know you not that you and I must dance,
  both our héels wrapt in a clout,
What mean you to make your houses gay,
And I must take the tenant away,
And dig for your sake the clods of clay?

Think you on the solemns Sizes past,
  how suddenly in Oxfordshire
I came and made the Judges all agast,
  and Justices that did appeare:
And tok both Bell and Baram away,
And many a worthy man that day,
And all their bodies brought to clay,

Think you that I dare not come to Schols,
  where all the cunning Clerks be most?
Take I not away both wise and fols?
  and am I not in every Coast?

Assure your selves no creature can
Make death affraid of any man,
Or know my coming where or when.

Where be they y make their leases strong,
  and joyn about them land to land?
Do you make account to live so long,
  to have the world come to your hand?
No foolish nowle, for all thy pence,
Full soon thy soul must néds go hence,
Then who shall toyl for thy defence?

And yon that lean on your Ladies Laps,
  and lay your heads upon their knée,
Think you for to play with Beautis paps,
  and not to come and dance with me?
No, fair Lords and Ladies all,
I will make you come when I do call,
And finde you a Pipe to dance withall.

And you that are busie-headed fols,
  to brabble for a pelting straw,
Know you not that I have ready tols
  to cut you from your crafty Law?
And you that falsely buy and sell,
And think you make your Markets well,
Must dance with death wheresoe'r you dwel.

Pride must have a pretty shéet, I sée,
  for properly she loves to dance,
Come away my wanton wench to me,
  as gallantly as your eye doth glance:
And all good fellows that slash and swash
In reds and yellows of revell dash,
I warrant you néd not be so rash.

For I can quickly cool you all,
  how hot or stout soever you bée,
Both high and low, both great and small,
  I nought do feare your high degrée:
The Ladies faire, the Beldames old,
The Champion stout, the Souldier bold,
Must all with me to earthly mold.

Therefore take time while it is lent,
  Prepare with me your selves to dance,
Forget me not, your lives lament,
  I come oft-times by sudden chance:
Be ready therefore, watch and pray,
That when my Minstrell Pipe doth play,
You may to Heaven dance the way.
                                  Finis.

Printed for F. Coles, J. Wright, T. Vere, and W. Gilbertson,

Pagâneſe

Figure 31 The 'Dance of Death' was painted on the walls of churches, including in the Guild Chapel of Stratford-upon-Avon, Shakespeare's home town. This painted panel was found in a building located on Broad Street in Oxford. The Medieval European 'Dance of Death' was a series of images showing death stealing away individuals from all walks of life, both men and women. AN.1990.101 © Ashmolean Museum, University of Oxford.

clumsily in his fight with Tybalt, Mercutio's dying curse on the play 'A plague o' both your houses' (3.1.91) predicts the destruction of both Capulet and Montague. In the context of early modern London its specific reference to plague must have sent a collective shiver down the audience's spine.

The prediction of the plague-hit families is ultimately realized in the final deadly tableau in the Capulet family monument. Like a plague, that is to say, the tragedy has robbed the two dynasties of their young. Dekker's *The Wonderful Year* includes the image of a grieving father holding the memory of a child killed by pestilence 'in the everlasting breast of Marble', rather like the statues raised to the lovers in the mourning Verona at the end of *Romeo and Juliet*.[14] Perhaps the 'star-crossed lovers' (Chorus 6) mentioned in the Prologue also allude, distantly, to one current theory that plague was caused by astrological coincidences.

Furthermore, the deaths of Romeo and Juliet are, indirectly, caused by plague. The Friar's careful choreography is interrupted when his messenger is trapped by 'the searchers of the town' 'in a house / Where the infectious pestilence did reign' (5.2.8–10). The reference would be obvious to members of the audience, who would have seen London houses closed up by searchers charged with identifying sites of infection and quarantining the inhabitants. The consequent failure to deliver the letter to Romeo explaining the plan of Juliet's feigned death is mortal: 'Unhappy fortune' indeed, as the Friar acknowledges (5.2.17). Before he can be intercepted, and thinking that his love is dead, Romeo acquires poison, makes his way to the tomb, and dies just as Juliet, on waking and seeing his corpse, kills herself with his dagger.

These are plague casualties at one remove. Perhaps that was close enough for Shakespeare and his plague-stressed audiences. Romeo and Juliet are the nearest victims of the all-present contemporary trauma – and the swiftness which shapes this whole drama is a version of and response to the terrifying rapidity of the onset of disease.

René Girard wrote in a famous essay that 'the distinctiveness of the plague is that it ultimately destroys all forms of distinctiveness'.[15] Mass burial pits for plague victims were one symbol of the way the disease erased social, gender and personal difference. Dekker noted that in the communal grave 'There friend foe, the young and old, / The freezing coward and the bold, / Servant and master, foul and fair / One livery wear, and fellows are.'[16] In *The Wonderful Year* he noted: 'I am amazed to remember what dead marches were made of three thousand together: husbands, wives and children being led as ordinarily to the grave as if they had gone to one bed.'[17] Dance-of-death imagery often shows Death moving obscenely among the living of all kinds and conditions, with them in the bedroom, at table, in the street as the personified version of this insidious threat (Figures 20 and 31). But, as Robert Watson observes, 'the anthropomorphizing of death – even when it is disguised as a grim surrender … is in fact a consoling fiction… The terror lies in its indifference, which steals away the differences by which and for which we live.'[18]

Shakespeare's later plays corroborate this attempt at consolation by emphasizing, through characterization and through dramaturgy, the unique and inerasable difference of his humans. The extended, choreographed moment of tragic death emphasizes the significance of the individual even as it seems to wipe him or her out. Elaborate plots, motives, interactions and obscurities focus our attention on the specificity of the human agents. No one, as we have seen, dies quickly, obscurely and disgustingly and is thrown into a communal grave. Rather, last words are given full hearing, epitaphs are soberly delivered, bodies taken off respectfully.

Fax mentis honestæ Gloria

HON SOY QVI MALY PENSE

HP HP

FAX MENTIS HONESTÆ . . IA

Iuuat ire per altum   Iuuat ire per altum

Crudeli crudaq Patri, patriaq, ruina
Raptus, ut ætherias insereretur auas:
HENRICVS modica Sanctu Caput vinditur Vrna;
Maximus Ille, suo ni genitore minor.
Hugo Hollandus fleuit

Whome all the vast frame of the fixed Earth
Shrunck vnder; now a weake Herse scarce bend:
His State he past in fact, in those his Partie:
His Youth in good life: & in Spirritt his Death.
Geo: Chapman

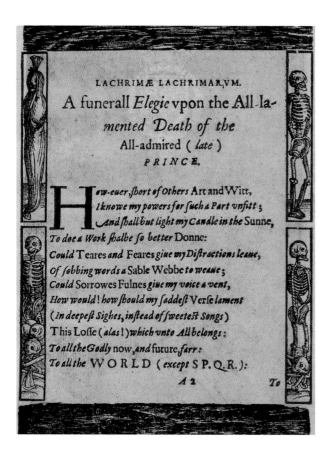

LACHRIMÆ LACHRIMARVM.

A funerall *Elegie* vpon the All-la-
mented *Death* of the
All-admired (*late*)
PRINCE.

How-euer, *short of Others* Art and Witt,
I knowe my powers for such a Part vnfitt;
And shall but light my Candle in the Sunne,
To doe a Work *shalbe so better* Donne:
Could Teares *and* Feares *giue my Distractions leaue,*
Of *sobbing words a* Sable Webbe *to weaue;*
Could Sorrowes Fulnes *giue my voice a vent,*
How *would! how should my saddest* Verse *lament*
(*In deepest Sighes, instead of sweetest Songs*)
This Losse (*alas!*) *which vnto* All *belongs:*
To all the Godly now, *and* future, *farr:*
To all the WORLD (*except* S P. Q. R.):
A 2   *To*

Death matters in Shakespeare's plays. By contrast to the plague's attack on distinctiveness, it is always individuated. Michael Neill has suggested that early modern tragedy is crucially about 'the discovery of death and the mapping of its meanings':[19] for Shakespeare, the evaded death represented by his own early escape from plague registered in a continued preoccupation with death's importance. If the plague elided human difference in its fatal ravages, his works rebuilt that individuality by using the moment of death as the supreme moment of autonomous self-realization.

Figures 32 and 33 The death of Prince Henry, James's heir, in 1612, was a cause of national mourning. Poems, music and other forms of commemoration made this the most elaborate communal spectacle of death in the period. *Opposite* Engraving of the tomb of Prince Henry, from *An epicede or funeral song, on the … death of … Henry prince of Wales,* by G. Chapman, London, 1612. Bodleian Library, 4° P 35(18) Th. *Above* Title page of *Lachrimae Lachrimarum,* by Josuah Sylvester, London 1612. Bodleian Library, J-J Sidney 135.

زبان بنواز نش فصاحت
هرآن کرد شنید درحال
چون هر دو یکجا بود بنوشت
انگشت کش سخن سرایان
کان سوخته و من زمانه
زان حال که بود زار زار کشت
نالید ز روی درد تا که
غلطید و مور خفته کرده
برداشت بسوی آسمان د
که نجست خوشیی و ا ر
این گفت و نهاد بر زمین سر
آن تربت را کشیده در بر

بی نیخت نمک بر آن جراحت
وان کند که بود تا بدین سال
دستوری خواست بازگشت

شد و منی از زشک دانه
بی روز تر و زار زار کشت
آمد سوی آن غریب خاکی
بنجید چو مار زخم خورده
انگشت کش ده دیده برد
در حفت یا رو در سلام

هایی دو سه مهر باقی با او
از قصه و قطعه و قصیده
وان جمله که گرفت بر باد

دستاس فلک شکسته خودش
جانی ز قدم رسیده نایب
در حلقه آن حظیره افتاد
پستی دو سر زار زار و خواند
کای خالق مه دِه افزود
آزاد کنم سنجت جا بی
چون تربت دوست در آ ورد

زان گونه که بود ساخت با او
یکی یکی بنوشت بر و بید
او ر دهبیه سوی بغداد
این قصه چنین برد پایان
چون کرد شکسته باد و رونش
روزی به ستم رسیده یاب
کشتیش در آب تر افتاد
اشکی دوست تلخ بنشاند
سوکند به برگزید ت
وابادکم سخت راضی
ای دوست بگفت دوست برادر

5

JOY OF THE WORM:
Death and Sex

One of the most common puns in Shakespeare's day was 'to die', or *petit mort*, the 'little death' of sexual abandonment or orgasm. As John Donne has it in 'The Good-Morrow': 'If our two loves be one, or, thou and I / Love so alike, that none do slacken, none can die.' The experience of sex involves a renunciation of the singular self, giving way to the 'mutual flame' of two lovers, or to a condition of porous dissolution in which humanness itself melts and liquefies. Here is Troilus, headily anticipating what it will be like when he finally gets to have sex with Cressida:

> I am giddy. Expectation whirls me round.
> Th'imaginary relish is so sweet
> That it enchants my sense. What will it be,
> When that the wat'ry palates taste indeed
> Love's thrice-repurèd nectar? Death, I fear me,
> Swooning destruction, or some joy too fine,
> Too subtle-potent, tuned too sharp in sweetness
> For the capacity of my ruder powers.
> I fear it much, and I do fear besides
> That I shall lose distinction in my joys,
> As doth a battle, when they charge on heaps
> The enemy flying.
>
> (*Troilus and Cressida*, 3.2.16–27)

Figure 34 The popular Arabic story of Layla and Majnun, illustrated here in a manuscript of the work of the twelfth-century Persian poet Nizami, shows how the telos of love, sex and death is a cross-cultural phenomenon. Bodleian Library, MS. Pers. d. 102, p. 105.

Sex gives a taste of death, perhaps its self-loss, perhaps its self-transcendence. The individual at once fulfils and exceeds herself. Troilus's fear that he 'shall lose distinction' in his joys is more than a fear of losing dignity in the ecstasy of sex. To 'lose distinction' is to lose recognizable form, as individuality is ceded to dispersal and violence. Troilus is very frankly imagining orgasm as one army charging and clambering over another army, all thoughts of serried files and hierarchy abandoned. Each individual soldier chases the 'enemy flying', hunting his own prize or pleasure, a great tumbling surge of appetite and terror spreading beyond the plain. The mixture of anonymous multitudes and individual panic equally characterizes sperm and battle, both observed as though from a vast distance. Either way, the result is death upon death upon death.

The famous opening to sonnet 129 puts it like this:

Th'expense of spirit in a waste of shame
Is lust in action

The 'waste' here is at once the spilled sperm, the entered woman, and a barren wasteland of expended 'spirit' and 'action' that is both spiritual and, through the implied metaphor, military. Desire generates death, as though by physical law. Public notions of decorum, reputation, policy don't stand a chance in the face of what the Greeks called *Eros* and *Thanatos*, humankind's foundational symbiosis.

As we have seen, this symbiosis thrums throughout *Measure for Measure*. From the play's outset, Claudio is marked with what that other son of Vienna, Sigmund Freud, would later identify as the death drive. In 'Beyond the Pleasure Principle' (1920) Freud examines the psychoanalytic distinction between 'ego-instincts and sexual instincts, and the view that the former exercises pressure towards death, and the latter towards a prolongation of life'.[20] For Claudio – and for the play itself – these instincts are confounded. As he is led away to prison in the first act of the play, Claudio identifies his sexual crime as a kind of suicidal desire:

> Our natures do pursue,
> Like rats that raven down their proper bane,
> A thirsty evil; and when we drink, we die.
>
> (1.2.120–22)

Sex here is transformed from its comedic associations with fertility into a tragic preoccupation with corruption. Protestant injunctions to 'be fruitful and multiply' have been perverted; sex is cognate with death rather than life. Mistress Overdone the Bawd has seen off nine husbands and is 'Overdone by the last' (2.1.195). At the end of the play, Angelo is forced to marry his erstwhile fiancée Mariana, but begs for a tragic, rather than a comic, ending:

> … I crave death more willingly than mercy.
> 'Tis my deserving, and I do entreat it.
>
> (5.1.475–6)

We hear the same association in more bawdy terms a moment later. Lucio's death sentence is commuted to marriage to Kate Keepdown, with whom he has an unwanted child: 'Marrying a punk, my lord, is pressing to death, whipping, and hanging' (521–2). There may be memories here of baroque sexual practices in the brothel. More pertinently, the torture is real, without promise of release: these are Lucio's final words. This is not the 'little death' of orgasm. It is a tormented sense that sex is mortal: humans are like insects for whom reproduction is death.

If sex is death-like, so too might death be sex-like – for the one who kills, and the one who dies. The act of killing can garner a terrible sexual supercharge. Othello smothers Desdemona on the unstained sheets of their marital bed, smelling and kissing her sleeping form as though the whole gruesome thing were a cleansing act of love. He then falls upon her corpse when he stabs himself, 'killing myself, to die upon a kiss', still ritualizing the slaughters as erotic atonements. Macbeth resolves to kill Duncan only when taunted by his wife as 'green and pale' in his 'love', a 'poor cat' afraid to match his 'act and valour' with his desire. He then imagines moving towards the sleeping king's bedchamber 'with Tarquin's ravishing strides'. The old man is figured as the innocent Lucrece, and every step of Macbeth's towards 'his design' a kind of rape.

The love story of *Romeo and Juliet* is always handcuffed to death. In Shakespeare's source-tale, the lovers enjoy a few months of surreptitious sex. Shakespeare cuts it to a single night, and this grabbed in the immediate wake of a crime that they both know has already foreshortened everything. The doom is upon them. We only see the lovers in the wake of their night together – a possible future that can never occur, that has passed before it came. The lovers are already subjects of nostalgia, aching for something that cannot return:

> *Juliet*   Wilt thou be gone? It is not yet near day.
> It was the nightingale, and not the lark,
> That pierced the fear-full hollow of thine ear.
> Nightly she sings on yond pom'granate tree.
> Believe me, love, it was the nightingale.
> *Romeo*   It was the lark, the herald of the morn,
> No nightingale.
>
> (3.5.1–7)

The bird of night is Juliet's, the bird of morn Romeo's. Their love belonged to night, but the night has passed. There is no space for it beneath the garish exposure of daylight. The nightingale is silent; the lark's song is their elegy. Either way, their love is indentured to death.

This is something that operatic translations of the story know very well. In Berlioz's version the lovers' words and passion are turned into orchestral music rather than arias or dialogue: their essence is to be beyond individuality. Similarly, Wagner's version of the story, *Tristan und Isolde*, reaches its climax with Isolde's 'Liebestod', her love-in-death song, which can only happen once her beloved is dead. For Romeo and Juliet, too, the consummation is absolute: the lovers *die*.

In *Antony and Cleopatra* the high Roman virtues, rooted in power, efficiency and public honour, are set against the deathly bliss and fascination of the Egyptians. Even the meanest tricks of Cleopatra tease with a need for death:

> Now I feed myself
> With most delicious poison.
>
> (1.5.26–7)

> Help me away, dear Charmian, I shall fall!
> It cannot be thus long – the sides of nature
> Will not sustain it.
>
> (1.3.15–17)

> O, my oblivion is a very Antony,
> And I am all forgotten.
>
> (91–2)

> But sir, forgive me,
> Since my becomings kill me when they do not
> Eye well to you.
>
> (96–8)

The phrase 'my becomings kill me' encapsulates the world of Cleopatra, in which every impulse is a little death, cherished the more the death is voluptuously shared. The cold politician Octavius diagnoses the same kind of spell at work everywhere. Here he is talking about the fickleness of popular affection, but he could equally be speaking of a middle-aged lover:

> This common body,
> Like to a vagabond flag upon the stream,
> Goes to, and back, lackeying the varying tide,
> To rot itself with motion.
>
> (1.4.44–7)

MORTALIA FACTA PERIBVNT

The sense is that every object in the world, whatever its function, is moved by the same death-enthralled rhythms. Pompey says much the same thing:

> But all the charms of love,
> Salt Cleopatra, soften thy waned lip. …
> Sharpen with cloyless sauce his appetite,
> That sleep and feeding may prorogue [defer] his honour
> Even till a Lethe'd dullness
>
> (2.1.20–27)

Antony is imagined as a kind of cow, battening mindlessly upon his lover to deathly oblivion (Lethe, the river of forgetfulness in the afterlife). Even in its delights, the body is coactive with death.

This way of living teases constantly with worldly shame – to which the only noble answer is suicide. Or this, at least, is the high Roman way. In this ideology, death serves the higher cause, which is honour (of the individual or of Rome). But in the world of the lovers, death is less a servant of a higher cause than an inspiration and aspiration. Hence the embarrassing confusions suffered by Antony when he is defeated by Caesar and betrayed, as he sees it, by Cleopatra. First he concludes that only one honourable path remains: 'There is left us / Ourselves to end ourselves (4.15.21–2). Then he vows to kill Cleopatra ('She hath betrayed me, and shall die the death', 4.15.26). He at once hears that Cleopatra has already killed herself, and is overcome by the need to meet her in death. He responds first by trying to will a heart attack ('O, cleave, my sides! / Heart, once be stronger than thy continent; / Crack thy frail case, 4.15.39–41) and then calls on his servant – aptly named Eros – to do the deed for him. Antony's sight is no longer on restoring his honour. It is entirely possessed by luxuriant visions of life in death:

> Eros! – I come, my queen. – Eros! – Stay for me.
> Where souls do couch on flowers we'll hand in hand,
> And with our sprightly port make the ghosts gaze.

> Dido and her Aeneas shall want troops,
> And all the haunt be ours. Come Eros, Eros!
>
> > (4.15.50–54)

Death is no tragedy. It is the resumption of play: bodilessness ('haunt', 'sprightly') becomes lustful possession. As Antony's self-pleasuring puns suggest, death is the ultimate erotic stage, an eternalizing scene of display. But Antony needs Eros to get him there. He begs his servant to cure him 'with a wound'; turns his back while Eros draws his sword; and is dismayed and rebuked when Eros kills himself instead, giving Antony 'brave instruction' in nobility. There is only one thing for it:

> But I will be
> A bridegroom in my death, and run into't
> As to a lover's bed.
>
> > (4.15.99–101)

He falls on his sword, but inexpertly:

> How, not dead? Not dead?...

And calls on his friends to finish the job:

> Let him that loves me strike me dead.
>
> *First Guard*   Not I!
> *Second Guard*   Nor I!
> *Third Guard*   Nor any one.
>
> > (108–9)

Like a punctured wheel, Antony remains, slowly expiring. He now discovers that Cleopatra is not dead after all. He is hauled aloft to her monument (a cumbersome exercise on stage), where he can breathe his last in her sight. His words fade away with his greatness: 'I am dying, Egypt, dying' (4.16.19, 43) he says twice, unable to raise himself to an appropriately memorable self-epitaph. Instead he passes with a final abject stab at wish fulfilment: 'a Roman by a Roman / Valiantly vanquished', he gasps, and then 'can no more' (4.16.59–61).

It is left to Cleopatra to find the words that were lost to her lover:

> O, withered is the garland of the war.
> The soldier's pole is fall'n.
>
> (4.16.66–7)

Antony's death is also the crumpling of male virility. It is now the queen to whom power is transferred – the power in and over death; the power of memorable poetry and of ritual. Initially she seems torn between different ways of dying, between mercurial escape and monumental sacrifice:

> Then is it sin
> To rush into the secret house of death
> Ere death dare come to us? …
> We'll bury him, and then what's brave, what's noble,
> Let's do it after the high Roman fashion,
> And make death proud to take us.
>
> (4.16.82–90)

Death, it seems, is being returned to decorum's safe keeping. And when Antony's death is reported to Caesar, the varnishing myths have already and depressingly begun:

> He is dead, Caesar,
> Not by a public minister of justice,
> Nor by a hirèd knife, but that self hand
> Which writ his honour in the acts it did
> Hath, with the courage which the heart did lend it,
> Splitted the heart.
>
> (5.1.19–24)

But in fact Cleopatra has other things in mind – an end more intimate with her desires:

> My desolation does begin to make
> A better life. 'Tis paltry to be Caesar. …
> And it is great
> To do that thing that ends all other deeds,
> Which shackles accidents and bolts up change
>
> (5.2.1–6)

Taken by Caesar's guards, her resolve hardens:

> Do Caesar what he can. Know sir, that I
> Will not wait pinioned at your master's court, …
> rather on Nilus' mud
> Lay me stark naked, and let the waterflies
> Blow me into abhorring
>
> (5.2.51–9)

She is in part returning to her origins, in which sex and extinction feed on one another like flies upon carrion flesh; and she is in part stealing from the marble grandeur of Rome, just as she stole their greatest soldier, designing a death scene that shall outface Caesar's plans to display her through Rome in triumph. First, she summons the fig man, who brings her 'the pretty worm / Of Nilus … that kills and pains not (5.2.238–9); then she calls for her robe and crown, to dress her 'Immortal longings' (5.2.275–6). Attired like this, met by the asp's kiss, she will once again greet Mark Antony:

> The stroke of death is as a lover's pinch,
> Which hurts and is desired. …
> Dost thou not see my baby at my breast,
> That sucks the nurse asleep? …

As sweet as balm, as soft as air, as gentle.
O Antony!

(5.2.290–92, 304–7)

And the Queen dies her very final death, just as the fig man wished it, flushed full with 'joy o'th' worm' (5.2.274).

6

DYING AGAIN:

English Histories

History plays are an extended exercise in artificial respiration, or in necromancy. In the theatrical magic of bringing the dead to life on stage, they challenge the boundaries between past and present and resuscitate long-dead heroes. For Thomas Nashe this dramatic raising of our forefathers from 'the grave of oblivion' could serve as 'a sharper reproof to these degenerate effeminate days of ours'. He elaborated, with reference to *1 Henry VI* (a play which he may well have had a hand in co-authoring): 'How would it have joyed brave Talbot, the terror of the French, to think that after he had lain two hundred years in his tomb, he should triumph again on the stage and have his bones new embalmed with the tears of ten thousand spectators at least.'[21] Talbot is brought from his grave onto the stage, revivified, but this resurrection is a cruel one. As Talbot is killed anew – 'the great Alcides of the field' 'Stinking and flyblown lies here at our feet' (*1 Henry VI*, 4.7.60, 76) – the play acknowledges that death cannot be evaded, only restaged.

Here, as across the plays, a parade of dead monarchs and nobles briefly revives, and dies again. In this sense, the defining, metonymic historical scene in Shakespeare is the visit of the ghosts of Richard's victims before the battle of Bosworth Field at the end of *Richard III*. In turn they address Richard and his nemesis Richmond, predicting their respective defeat and victory in the play's final encounter. In fact, all the characters of *Richard III* have the same spectral quality of

the already-dead: Richard himself is as ghostly as his murdered brother Clarence. Theatre, particularly historical theatre, is always ghostly: Stephen Greenblatt calls it 'a cult of the dead'.[22] Marvin Carlson's study of *The Haunted Stage* takes as an epigraph for the whole spooky ontology of performance Marcellus's nervy remark on the battlements of Elsinore: 'What, has this thing appeared again tonight?' (*Hamlet*, 1.1. 19)[23] History is the preferred genre of the revenant.

The double-time scheme of many history plays, in which what is predicted within the fiction is the already-known historical past for the audience, gives them a particular freedom simultaneously to present their characters as alive and as dead. The infant Elizabeth who appears and is apostrophized as 'a pattern to all princes living with her' at the end of *Henry VIII* was already entombed in Westminster Abbey by the time the play was performed at the Globe in 1613. This dual movement – resurrecting the dead in order to kill them again for our entertainment, and looping past, present and future in dizzying ways – establishes the uncanny coordinates of Shakespeare's historical dramaturgy during the 1590s.

The 1590s in England was a decade at war: in the Netherlands, in France and, most pressingly, in Ireland. The long military campaign in Ireland, memorably dubbed by one historian 'England's Vietnam',[24] received fresh impetus in the spring of 1599, when the Earl of Essex led a gallant company of soldiers out of London, confident of decisive victory. It is a moment caught, suspended, in the most topical lines in all of Shakespeare's works: the Chorus to Act 5 of *Henry V*, written in the same year. Imagine the popular

Figures 39 and 40 Lydgate's *Fall of Princes* offered a late-medieval paradigm for the monarchical tragedies of Shakespeare and his contemporaries. Bodleian Library, MS. Bodl. 263, p. 7 (after 1439) and a printed edition of 1554. Douce L240, titlepage. The latter edition (figure 40) was owned by William Herbert, Shakespeare's patron.

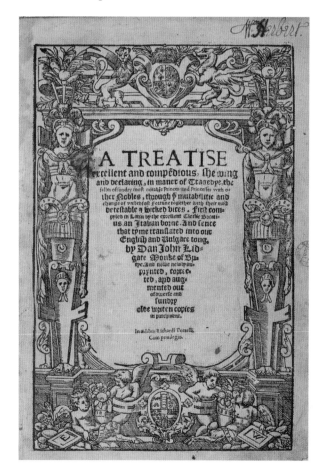

response at Henry's successful return from his French wars of conquest, the Chorus invites, using a parallel with a fantasy victory rather closer to home:

As, by a lower but high-loving likelihood,
Were now the General of our gracious Empress –
As in good time he may – from Ireland coming,
Bringing rebellion broachèd on his sword,
How many would the peaceful city quit
To welcome him!   (5.0.29–34)

The play imagines Essex victorious in Ireland – and incidentally attests to the short, specific theatrical runs characteristic of early modern theatre programming. *Henry V* was apparently performed in the late spring and early summer of 1599, after Essex's chivalric departure but before the disastrous outcome of his expedition was known. His inglorious return, just three months after his famous departure, was recorded by the historian William Camden: at 'the latter end of July, with his soldiers wearied, sickly, and their number more than a man would believe, diminished'.[25]

Like the story of Essex's fateful expedition, the contemporaneous play *Henry V* entertains both possibilities: glorious victory and ignominious defeat. One critic has influentially deployed the optical illusion that simultaneously reveals a rabbit and a duck as a metaphor for this double effect. The play reveals with particular clarity the knowledge that behind victory is loss, and that wars bring casualties as well as conquests. Overly patriotic productions that minimize this understanding do so by cutting the play extensively: Laurence Olivier's wartime film, for example, cut more than half the play. The cost of wars of the 1590s has been calculated by one modern historian with a striking comparison: 'Elizabethan losses during the war period [were] about *fifty* times worse than American casualties in Vietnam.'[26] Most of these Elizabethan soldiers were recruited from the lower classes. In *2 Henry IV* we see this process depicted on stage, with Falstaff as the cynical recruiting sergeant assessing the patently inadequate Ralph Mouldy, Simon Shadow, Thomas Wart, Francis Feeble and Peter Bullcalf as potential conscripts for Henry's civil wars. Battle, like the rest of society, was socially stratified. Its dangers were greater for the lower-status foot soldier than for the gentleman captains.

Henry V struggles with the contradictory impulses to glorify and to interrogate war. The play's Chorus does double duty as – in modern terms – a kind of spin doctor or patriotic embedded reporter. While the Chorus constantly reminds us that theatrical representation is inadequate to the scale of the battle of 'two mighty monarchies', it also consistently asserts Henry's own nobility as 'the mirror of all Christian kings'. The Chorus to Act 4, on the eve of the battle of Agincourt, is particularly relevant here, as it depicts the 'poor condemned English' contemplating the 'morning's danger' comforted by their 'royal captain' 'with cheerful semblance and sweet majesty' and 'a little touch of Harry in the night'.

But in one of the play's many delicate ironies, the unfolding scenes which follow do not quite bear out this positive reading. Henry, disguised, meets three soldiers. They are unusually given full names as if to register their individual significance: John Bates, Alexander Court and Michael Williams. These are ordinary men, not the caricatures indicated by the names Mouldy and Wart, Falstaff's hapless conscripts, nor the Cobbler and Carpenter who represent the citizens of Rome in the contemporaneous *Julius Caesar*.

Far from being comforted by his words, these ordinary men in the English camp articulate the reality behind the king's rhetoric of brotherhood. Their fear of death is real, cold and heartfelt. They know that they are cannon fodder, likely to be killed while the king is ultimately safe, likely to be ransomed. And they worry away at this play's ethical scab that will not stop itching: the question of the morality of Henry's claim to the French throne:

> if the cause be not good, the King himself hath a heavy reckoning to make, when all those legs and arms and heads, chopped off in a battle, shall join together at the latter day, and cry all, 'We died at such a place' – some swearing, some crying for a surgeon, some upon their

HYBERNIÆ, etc. RICHARDVS TERTVS ANGLIÆ ET FRANCIA REX DOMINVS

The portraict of RICHARD the 3. King of England, and Fraunce,
Lord of Ireland. He was slaine at Bosworth feild. the 22th of August.
1486. and homelye buried at the Graye friers Church in Leicester. when he
had usurped 2 yeares 2 monthes and one day

Are to be sold by Compton Holland over against the Exchange.

This impression was
seal of Richard the
was dug up some yeares
Fiield. and fell into
late Dr Lort.   EM.

taken from the
Third. which
age in Bosworth
the hand of the
Above was
Richards cognizance.

THE
TRAGEDIE
of King Richard
the third.

Containing his treacherous Plots against his brother Clarence: the pittifull murther of his innocent Nephewes: his tyrannicall vsurpation: with the whole course of his detested life, and most deserued death.

As it hath beene lately Acted by the Kings Maiesties seruants.

Newly augmented,

By William Shake-speare.

LONDON,

Printed by Thomas Creede, and are to be sold by Mathew Lawe, dwelling in Pauls Church-yard, at the Signe of the Foxe, neare S. Austins gate, 1 6 1 2.

[The above date is undoubtedly 1612]

wives left poor behind them, some upon the debts they owe, some upon their children rawly left. I am afeard there are few die well that die in a battle

(*Henry V*, 4.1.133–41)

The notion of bodily resurrection familiar from the Elizabethan pulpit is here twisted to express a Hieronymous Bosch-style vision of severed limbs joining in grotesque condemnation of Henry's warmongering.

Henry's response to this moral challenge is threefold. He angrily challenges Williams to a fight if they both survive the battle, and the combatants exchange gloves. He retreats into private prayer, where he tries to suggest that the lot of a king is nevertheless much worse than that of a commoner. No king, burdened with the cares of state and 'laid in bed majestical, / Can sleep so soundly as the wretched slave / Who with a body filled and vacant mind / Gets him to rest' (4.1.264–7): having just come from the sleepless soldiers haunted by their own likely deaths, the comparison seems crassly self-indulgent. And he addresses his men the next day in famously stirring terms that suggest shared danger will level their social disparities:

> We few, we happy few, we band of brothers.
> For he today that sheds his blood with me,
> Shall be my brother; be he ne'er so vile,
> This day shall gentle his condition.
>
> (4.3.60–63)

Figure 41 *previous page* Many of the Bodleian's early quartos of Shakespeare are from the collection of Edmond Malone. His annotations to this 1612 edition of *Richard III* add a piece of historical verisimilitude to Shakespeare's play: 'This impression was taken from the seal of Richard the Third, which was dug up some years ago in Bosworth Field'. Bodleian Library, Arch. G d.39 (6).

Addressing the audience in the Globe Theatre as well as the onstage troops, Henry shames those men who have not enlisted to fight:

> And gentlemen in England now abed
> Shall think themselves accursed they were not here
>
> (64–5)

The unsettling encounter with Bates, Williams and Court shapes Henry's preparation for Agincourt and makes him articulate the contradictions of royal privilege.

Those contradictions are amplified when the news of the casualties reaches him after Agincourt. The Herald brings an account of the ten thousand French dead, listed by rank:

> Of princes in this number
> And nobles bearing banners, there lie dead
> One hundred twenty-six; added to these,
> Of knights, esquires and gallant gentlemen,
> Eight thousand and four hundred.
>
> (4.8.81–5)

It is, Henry notes, 'a royal fellowship of death'. The English casualties are listed in the same hierarchical way:

> Edward the Duke of York, the Earl of Suffolk,
> Sir Richard Keighley, Davy Gam Esquire;
> None else of name, and of all other men
> But five-and-twenty.
>
> (103–6)

The anonymous twenty-five war dead who are 'none else of name' do not appear to have had their condition gentled by fighting with the king. Rather it is his blood brother, Edward Duke of York, who heads the roll-call, which apparently omits any of that 'band of brothers' he addressed so movingly before the charge. The play stages the uneasy reunion of Williams and the King in the aftermath of the battle, but we do not know whether his frightened comrades Bates and Court survive.

Not surprisingly, given the play's careful ironies and contradictions here, *Henry V* has often been read as an anti-war play. Reviews of a 1941 production in Regent's Park, for instance, praised its sympathy for the 'common soldier';[27] the poet David

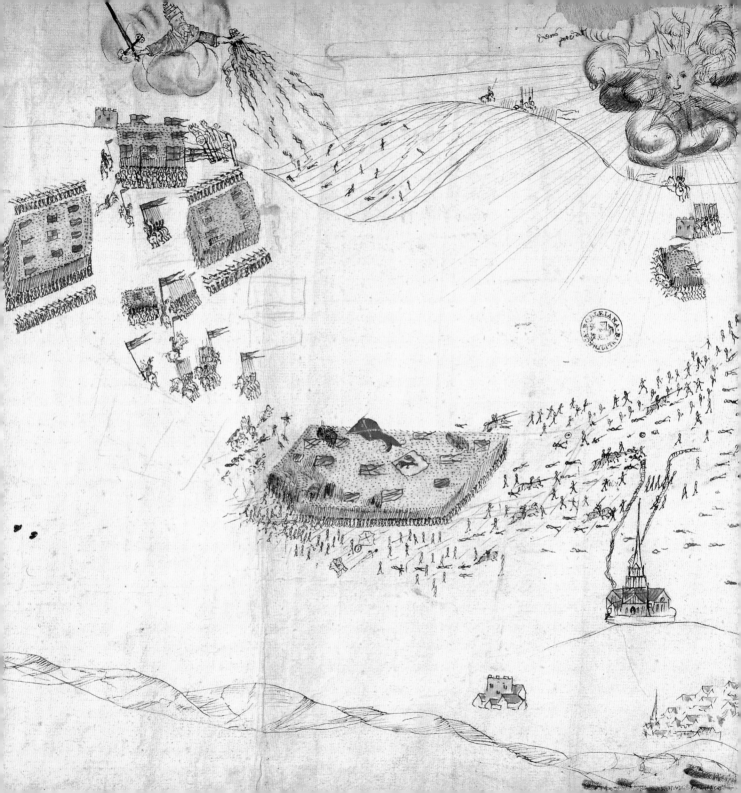

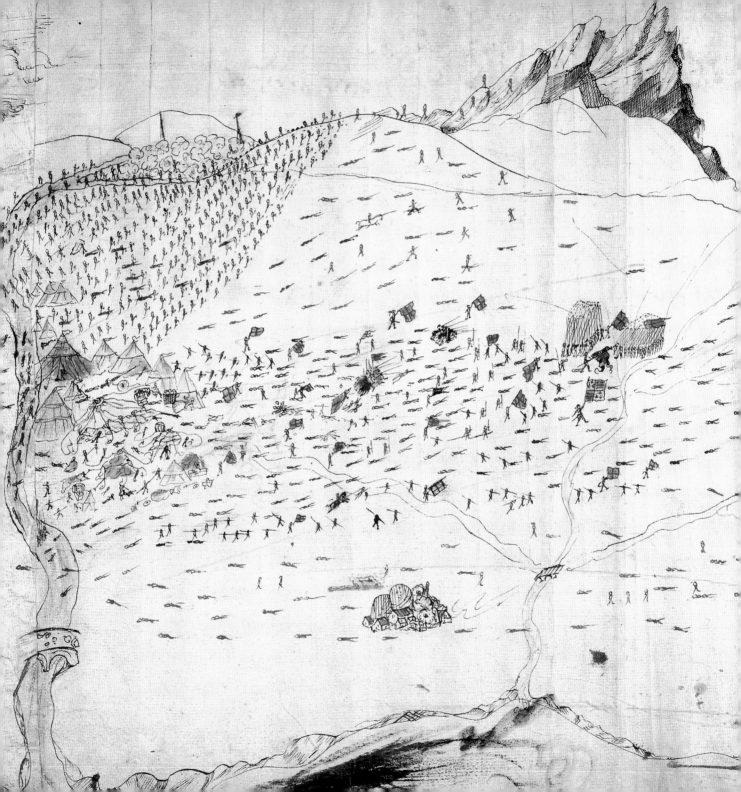

Jones identified his own wartime experiences not in the play's heroics but in the detail of its apparently marginal characters – 'Bardolph's marching kiss for Pistol's "quondam Quickly" is an experience substantially the same as you and I suffered on Victoria platform.'[28] A deeply ambiguous production of the play directed by Nicholas Hytner against the backdrop of the contested UK–American war in Iraq in 2003 had Henry and Catherine's wooing scene set amid body bags of the fallen.

Henry himself, and his Chorus, want to be in a heroic play, but what Shakespeare writes for them is more nuanced, more ironic, more conscious of the costs of war, particularly for the ordinary soldier. The play ends not with the English victory against the odds at Agincourt, nor with the success of its surprising lurch towards romantic comedy in the final scene, but with an Epilogue telling us of Henry's early death, and the loss of France under his infant heir, which 'made his England bleed' (Epilogue 12). Even survival in a history play is merely a temporary reprieve from the condition of history: to be already dead. Five years before *Henry V* was performed at the Globe, Shakespeare's company had been playing the next historical episode. *1 Henry VI* had begun with Henry V's funeral. *Henry V* may attempt to be a feel-good play for a London weary of war, a cheerleader for Essex's inevitable success in Ireland, but it is ultimately shot through with realism: 'few die well that die in a battle' (4.1.40–41).

It's a sentiment Shakespeare's vital anti-hero Falstaff lives by – literally. Shakespeare's history plays habitually give us, in Richard II's words, 'sad stories on the death of kings'. This genre is particularly attentive to time passing, the historical wheel turning, as one generation is eclipsed by the next. The king is dead, long live the king. Death is not an end point in the genre of history play as it is in the adjacent genre of tragedy, but it is still inevitable. When the two old men, Silence and Shallow, reminisce in *2 Henry IV*, their conversation is all about mortality: 'to see how many of my old acquaintance are dead', Shallow muses. 'Death, as the Psalmist saith, is certain to all; all shall die' (3.1.33–6).

When we first meet Falstaff in the second scene of *1 Henry IV*, the prince teases him for wanting to know the time: 'What a devil hast thou to do with

Mors est hic hoi semp cum tpe labi. Et semp quadã 2ditiõe Mozi Est hois nudũ nasci nu=
dũqz reuerti. Est homnis putrere solo limõqz fateri. Et miseris gradibus in cinerẽ redigi.
Res 7 opes przstantur / 7 famulantur ad hozam. Et locuplex mane vespere pauper erit.

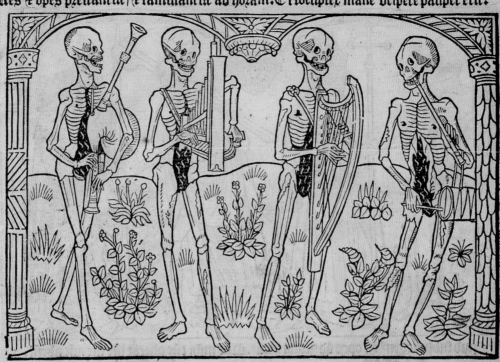

Omnia cesar erat 7 glozia cesaris esse desinit / 7 tumulus bix exa octo pedum.

Le przmier mozt.	Le tiers mozt.
¶Uous qui par diuine sentence	¶Entendez ce que ie bous ditz
Qui biuez en estatz diuers	Jeunes 7 bieulx petis 7 grans
Tous denserez en ceste danse	De iour en iour selon les ditz
Une fois 7 bons 7 peruers	Des saiges bous allez mourans
Et si serons mengez de bers	Car bous cueurs bont diminuant
Uoz cozps / helas regardez nous	Pourquoy tous serez trespassez
Mozs / porris / puans descouuers	Ceulx qui biuent deuant cent ans
Comme sommes telz seres bous.	Las cent ans seront tost passez
Le second mozt.	¶Le quart mozt.
¶Dicl es nous par quelles raisons	¶Deuant quil soyent cent ans passez
Uous ne pensez point a mourir	Tous les biuans comme ie dis
Quant la mozt ba en boz maison	De ce monde seront passez
Huy lung / demain laultre querir	En enfer ou en paradis
Sans quon bous puisse secourir	Mon compaignon / mais ie te ditz
Cest mal bescu de ny penser	Peu de gens sont qui ayent cure
Et trop grant danglier de perir	Des trespassez ne de noz ditz
Force est quil faille ainst denser.	Le fait deulx gist en auanture.

the time of the day?' (1.2.6) Falstaff is a creature outside time and its confines, but by the end of *Part 2* the old knight, too, is time-bound: 'We have heard the chimes at midnight' (3.2.211). But although Falstaff ages across the plays, he is also a lively challenge to the assumptions of the history play, a genre in which he only partly belongs. His character was originally called 'Oldcastle', representing a historical knight who accompanied Henry IV in his wars and was martyred for Lollardy in the reign of Henry V. Oldcastle was pictured as a Protestant hero by John Bale in 1544 (Figure 46), and in the extensive graphic history of the Reformation by John Foxe, *Acts and Monuments* (better known as Foxe's *Book of Martyrs*) (Figure 4), Foxe suggested as part of his anti-Catholic calendar that Oldcastle should be annually commemorated as a Protestant saint on 5 February. Why Shakespeare would so shift Oldcastle's representation from this pious figure of Protestant prehistory to the witty, weighty and self-interested character of his own history plays is unclear. What is evident, however, is that the powerful Elizabethan descendants of John Oldcastle did not appreciate the rewriting: the late change to the name Falstaff appears to have been a response to their disapproval.

But calling the play's central anti-hero by this unhistoric name is also a freedom, and a freedom Falstaff himself exploits. His fatness symbolizes his larger-than-life qualities: he is too big to fail. On the battlefield at Shrewsbury he rewrites his own history, carrying a bottle of sack in place of a weapon, and ducking out of the conventional heroics of war, noting sardonically that 'Honour is a mere scutcheon': 'What is that "honour"? Air. A trim reckoning! Who hath it? He that died o' Wednesday. Doth he feel it? No. Doth he hear it? No. 'Tis insensible then? Yea. To the dead' (*1 Henry IV*, 5.1.34–40). Falstaff's scepticism is a challenge to history-play values, as is his recognition that the conscripted soldiers are merely some one hundred and fifty 'cankers of a calm world and a long peace' (4.2.30–34). They are but 'food for powder, food for powder. They'll fill a pit as well as better. Tush, mortal men, mortal men' (65–7), in a shockingly callous reminder that civil war is fuelled by a sense that ordinary life is cheap.

Figure 44 Dürer's famous print of the Four Horsemen of the Apocalypse combines the iconography of the Dance of Death with the symbolism of the Book of Revelation: the Chorus to *Henry V* seems to recall this when it imagines 'famine, sword and fire' 'crouch[ing] for employment'. Bodleian Library, Douce D subt. 41 (fol 57).

Deo gracias anglia redde pro victoria Owre kynge went

forth to normandy. With grace & myyt of chyualry: þer god for hym wrouyt meruelusly

Wherfore englonde may calle & cry: Deo gracias.

Chorus:

Deo gracias anglia redde pro victoria.

He sette a sege þe sothe for to say
to harflu towne with ryal aray
þat towne he wan & made a fray
þat fraunce shal rywe tyl domesday.
Deo gracias.

Then went owre kynge with alle his oste
þorowe fraunce for alle þe frenshe boste
he spared no drede of lest ne moste
tyl he come to agincourt coste.
Deo gracias.

Then forsoth þat knyt comely
in agincourt feld he faut manly
þorow grace of god most myyty
he had boþe þe felde & þe victory.
Deo gracias.

Ther dukys & erlys lorde & barone
were take & slayne & þat wel sone
and summe were ladde in to lundone
with ioye and merthe & grete renone.
Deo gracias.

Now gracious god he saue owre kynge
his peple & alle his wel wyllynge
gef hym gode lyfe & gode endynge
þat we with merth mowe saufely synge.
Deo gracias.

I rede þat þou be mery whyl þou mowe ...

She seyt on fonde. þat lady þus so lowely. hos semblaunt was so semely ...
of alle my care & doutte she may my balis bete.
by here oste & ceruant yat serdes al in hir care.
he denyed by his semblaunt a man of þe olde ...
I wondryst he seide ... skylfully. in synge þat haft be holde
And þy þyke tyskly. tyl taky r keyse me y toke.

The story of the historic Sir John Oldcastle was, like all martyr narratives, heavily teleological, retrospectively shaped by his defining death. Foxe's illustration showed Oldcastle's 'cruel martyrdom' in a woodcut framed by a kind of gallows to which the naked victim was chained, writhing in the flames, hemmed in by armed men and a close-packed crowd. Oldcastle's vital avatar Falstaff would have none of this. At the end of *1 Henry IV*, two pairs of hand-to-hand combatants coincide on the battlefield at Shrewsbury. Prince Henry meets the chivalric and impulsive Henry Percy, Hotspur, with whom he has been unfavourably compared from the play's beginning; Falstaff is cornered by the brave Scot Douglas. Readers of the Quarto text, in which this most popular play was reprinted from 1598 onwards, were given an explanation in a stage direction of the different outcome of these two contests: '*Enter Douglas, he fighteth with Falstaffe, he fals down as if he were dead, the Prince killeth Percy*'. The historic Percy's life bleeds away in the dirt: 'food for – worms', as the Prince observes. The ahistoric Falstaff feigns death and lives to fight (or not) another day. After the stage has cleared, Falstaff judges it safe to emerge, and the stage direction '*Falstaffe riseth up*' gives an almost mythic sense of his irrepressible resurrection. The better part of valour', as he observes, 'is discretion, in the which better part I have saved my life' (5.4.118–20).

The feigning of death on stage fascinates Shakespeare. This is in part because all deaths in plays are, of course, ultimately feigned. In performances of *1 Henry IV* it may have been less evident that Falstaff was merely playing dead: audiences then, as now, may have trained themselves to ignore the rising chest of the actor who has 'died' in a bout of physical exertion and whose living presence on the stage contradicts his fictional death. Characters may die, but actors do not. The deaths on stage are recuperated as entertainment because they have not actually happened. And Falstaff's feigned death is a comic anticipation of other manipulations of the border between living and dying and of the audience's willingness to accept the fiction of death on stage, including the deaths of Desdemona in *Othello*, Cordelia at the end of *King Lear*, Innogen in *Cymbeline*, and Hermione in *The Winter's Tale*.

Figure 45 The fifteenth-century Agincourt carol recounts Henry's victory, acknowledging only enemy casualties: 'Ther dukys and erlys lorde and barone / Were taken and slayne and that wel sone', with a chorus 'Deo gratias Anglia redde pro victoria' [England, give thanks to God for victory] Bodleian Library, MS. Arch. Selden. B. 26, fols. 17v–18r.

Figure 46 Shakespeare's disreputable fat knight Sir John Falstaff originally had the name of this historical figure, Sir John Oldcastle. Oldcastle was executed in 1417 for his part in a Lollard uprising, and was considered by Protestants a martyr. Falstaff resists both the piety of Oldcastle and his martyred death, pretending death in the battlefield at Shrewsbury to avoid injury. *A brefe chronicle concernynge the examinacyon and death of the blessed martyr of Christ syr Iohan Oldecastell the lorde Cobham*, 1544. Bodleian Library, Mal. 503.

Prince Henry's brusque eulogy over Falstaff's apparent bulky corpse 'I could have better spared a better man' (5.4.103) similarly anticipates the many moving but ultimately ironic elegies in later plays where the dead turn out not to be, and the mourning of the living is curiously or pre-emptively misdirected. But here in *1 Henry IV* it also has a specific generic function. Falstaff seems uniquely able to step out of the historical inevitability that shapes the destinies of other characters. He can reappear in a quite different world, contemporary bourgeois Windsor, in *The Merry Wives of Windsor*, and again in *2 Henry IV*, the sequel spawned by his own enormous popularity. The end of that play sees him again in danger: this time psychological rather than physical. Rejected by his former companion Prince,

now King, Henry, Falstaff again chooses the passive course: as at Shrewsbury he withdraws himself from the confrontation, reassuring the others 'I shall be sent for in private to him' (*2 Henry IV*, 5.5.76).

The play's Epilogue continues the reassurance that Falstaff is a character who will return, 'our humble author will continue the story with Sir John in it', remarking snidely, 'for anything I know, Falstaff shall die of a sweat – unless already a be killed with your hard opinions. For Oldcastle died a martyr, and this is not the man' (25–30). That Falstaff repudiates the death drive of martyrdom and continues, irrepressible, across three plays, differentiates him entirely from Oldcastle: his character is defined – like that of *Measure for Measure*'s Barnardine, discussed in Chapter 2 – by his refusal to die. The fact that in *Henry V* he is now 'in Arthur's bosom' shows the later play's return to the genre of history: for this play, as for Prince Henry himself, the fun is over. The ludic has been decisively overwritten by the politic; the chimes at midnight are fading; 'all shall die'.

Figure 47 *previous page* This nineteenth-century image from *Henry IV* shows Falstaff amid the battle dead, peeping out from under a shield, as Hotspur and Prince Hal meet at last. Engraving after Francis Rigaud, from *A collection of prints, from pictures painted [for the Shakespeare gallery of John and Josiah Boydell]*, 1803. (v.2), Bodleian Library, Johnson a.59.

7

ANOTHER GOLGOTHA:

Places of Death

There is much about the basic physical fabric of Shakespeare's stage that makes it appropriate for the staging of death. His company called their best-known playhouse 'The Globe' for good traditional reasons. Since medieval times the theatre had presented itself as a microcosm, a miniature model of the great cosmic geography, suitable for stories that dramatized the path through life to eternal judgement. This did not depend upon permanent theatres (the first such structure in London was not built until the late 1570s). Any space – church, courtyard, street, house – might be adapted to performance through the simple expedient of setting-up 'stations' or 'mansions' representing specific locations, often biblical or metaphysical, working inside a more fluid space of actor and audience interaction. These stations – which might be rendered by a booth or a cart, a rudimentary hanging or picture or model – would typically represent places such as Heaven, Hell's mouth, Jerusalem, or Pilate's palace. In other words, the theatrical spectacle could actually present the world beyond this world; the space of death could be physically, symbolically actualized. Shakespeare's theatre was a more secular affair, but the same associations could always be tapped into. The roof above was still called the 'heavens'; the wooden boards were bare and stark, a potentially desolate space in which the actor might at any moment feel himself terrifyingly isolated, alone or not, facing the fact of

Figure 48 Hamlet in the graveyard has become the play's iconic scene: the bones disturbed by the digging of Ophelia's grave prompt a disgust at the putrid, desiccated physicality of death that becomes a disgust at life itself. Eugene Delacroix, *Hamlet and Horatio in the graveyard*, 1835. Städelsches Kunstinstitut, Franfurt, Germany. Image © Peter Horree/ Alamy.

judgement – if not the judgement of heaven, then of those waiting executioners, the audience:

> As in a theatre the eyes of men,
> After a well-graced actor leaves the stage,
> Are idly bent on him that enters next,
> Thinking his prattle to be tedious,
> Even so, or with much more contempt, men's eyes
> Did scowl on gentle Richard. No man cried 'God save him!'
> No joyful tongue gave him his welcome home;
> But dust was thrown upon his sacred head
>
> (*Richard II*, 5.2.23–30)

The stage wasn't called a 'scaffold' for nothing. And these bare boards gave way to a trapdoor that could stand either for a grave, or purgatory, or hell.

It is perhaps no surprise that Shakespeare often associated the simple fact of playing with the still more simple fact of passing away. As Juliet has it, 'My dismal scene I needs must act alone' (*Romeo and Juliet*, 4.3.19) Again and again his characters see themselves as actors, and in the same movement as temporary pawns, fated to appear and disappear in the blink of a spectator's eye:

> Life's but a walking shadow, a poor player
> That struts and frets his hour upon the stage,
> And then is heard no more.
>
> (*Macbeth*, 5.5.23–5)

Another word for a player was a 'shadow' – a non-body, essentially insubstantial, a condition that comes truest in its own disappearance:

> Thus play I in one person many people,
> And none contented. Sometimes am I king;
> Then treason makes me wish myself a beggar,

And so I am. Then crushing penury
Persuades me I was better when a king.
Then am I kinged again, and by and by
Think that I am unkinged by Bolingbroke,
And straight am nothing.

(*Richard II*, 5.5.31–8)

As Jaques famously has it in *As You Like It*, 'All the world's a stage, / And all the men and women merely players. / They have their exits and their entrances', culminating in the 'Last scene of all, / That ends this strange, eventful history': 'mere oblivion, / Sans teeth, sans eyes, sans taste, sans everything' (2.7.139–66). Jaques here moves almost imperceptibly from the indignities of old age to the still greater depredations of being-in-death itself.

The archetypal scene here is Hamlet in the graveyard. 'How long will a man lie i'th' earth ere he rot?' (5.1.159) he asks the gravedigger, leading to the discovery of the skull of his old playmate, the jester Yorick:

My gorge rises at it. Here hung those lips that I have kissed I know not how oft. ... Quite chop-fallen? Now get you to my lady's chamber and tell her, let her paint an inch thick, to this favour she must come. Make her laugh at that.

(*Hamlet*, 5.1.183–90)

Hamlet's disgust at the putrid, desiccated physicality of death becomes a disgust at life. The jewels of life – things like laughter and beauty – become the masks and property of death, as all animation is turned into a hideous pretence.

At this particular moment Hamlet's death thoughts are reinforced by physical props and stage technology – the skull representing Yorick, the trapdoor standing for the grave being dug. But as much as the visible image has become iconic – the young prince cradling or staring into the sockets of a skull – this physically actualized symbolism is also unusual. Props and back-hangings could occasionally do effective work, but in the main the boards of the stage stayed bare. Moreover,

Figure 49 Eric Gill's illustration of the play's final scene for a 1933 limited edition of *Hamlet* is placed just before the graveyard, as if in recognition that this encounter with Yorick and with mortality is the play's endpoint, not the final denoument of its plot. Bodleian Library, M. adds. 65 e.63.

ne 7

ou, poor Ophelia,
ears: but yet
ustom holds,
   when these are gone,
ieu, my lord:
   fain would blaze,

alm his rage!
start again;

Act V. Scene 1. A Churchyard. Enter two Clowns, with spades, etc.

1st C.   **IS** HE to be buried in Christian burial that wilfully seeks her own salvation?
2nd C.   I tell thee she is; and therefore make her grave straight: the crowner hath sat on her, and finds it Christian burial.
1st C.   How can that be, unless she drowned herself in her own defence?
2nd C. Why, 'tis found so.

sight-enhancing eyewear was rare; and any groundling beneath average height might struggle to see what was happening up on the stage. Consequently, it was *words* that had to do the job of generating pictures. So it is as the graveyard scene progresses. Hamlet exemplifies a truly Shakespearean imagination – one that will not stop, that travels far beyond what can be seen into the unsightly realities of existing:

> Why may not imagination trace the noble dust of Alexander till a find it stopping a bung-hole?
>
> > (5.1.198–200)

The sturdy Horatio rebukes his friend for being morbidly fanciful ("Twere to consider too curiously to consider so'), but it is Hamlet who is the truer guide to the terrain spanned by these plays:

> Imperial Caesar, dead and turned to clay,
> Might stop a hole to keep the wind away.
>
> > (5.1.201, 208–9)

Death is no metaphysical abstraction. It is here, now, everywhere, feeding upon life. *Hamlet*'s understanding of death is preoccupied with the physical rather than the spiritual. Hamlet and Laertes fight in Ophelia's grave; the prince's attitude to the corpse of Polonius is the brusque 'I'll lug the guts into the neighbour room' (3.4.186); Alexander's 'noble dust' is to be found bunging the hole in a barrel. But life also builds upon death. Hamlet's blackly comic fantasy – Caesar's degraded corpse being used as building mortar to keep out the wind – shows death employed in the service of precarious physical comfort. In Shakespeare, death is always coming home. There is no life without it.

We can see in Hamlet's mordant rhyme how death might be lurking anywhere, awake or asleep. Shakespeare builds entire tragic worlds out of this fact. A case in point is *Macbeth*. Almost everything in this play bears the mark of death. This fact is cued by the appearance of the witches, whose seeming foreknowledge has the

Figure 50 Eighteenth-century editions of Shakespeare often condensed the play's action to a single illustration: here it is the interpretation of Caesar's corpse that stands in for the play *Julius Caesar*. Bodleian Library. Percy 56.

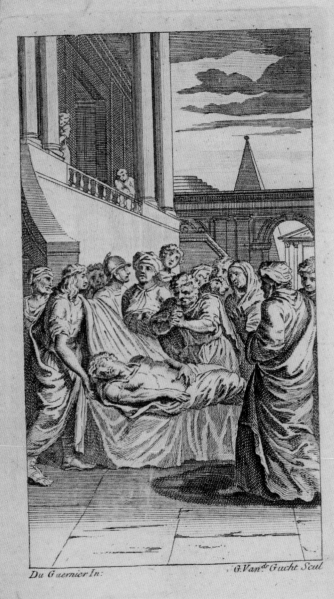

Du Guernier In: G. Van.dr Gucht Scul

JULIUS CÆSAR.

A

TRAGEDY.

As it is Acted at the

THEATRE ROYAL.

IN DRURY-LANE.

By His MAJESTY's Servants.

By WILLIAM SHAKESPEAR.

LONDON:

Printed for J. and R. TONSON and S. DRAPER.
in the *Strand*,

MDCCLI.

effect of making present events feel as though they have already happened, or that the agent enacting them is a kind of sleepwalker, performing deeds that someone or something else has set in motion. As Lady Macbeth says, 'I feel now / The future in the instant' (1.5.56–7). Time is concertinaed; the present is vaporized; death is already here. It can feel as though characters arrive at a killing field that already bears its dead – and proceed to kill them all over again. As the Captain reports:

> Except they meant to bathe in reeking wounds
> Or memorize another Golgotha,
> I cannot tell –
>
> (1.2.39–41)

They are washed in the blood and steam of those they have killed, as though born from it, or baptized in it. The religious connotations are reinforced by 'another Golgotha': this refers to Calvary, the hill where Christ and the murderers were crucified; more specifically, it means the place of dead men's skulls. To 'memorize' such another horror is to commit it to memory, and to do so through violent repetition, cut upon cut, wound upon wound, skull upon skull, like the most terrible education imaginable. History, memory, mind itself, is an accumulation of killings. The result is this play-world and its Scotland: a place of unhoused skulls, a hill of skulls that the action contributes to and proceeds upon. The basic conditions of the *Macbeth* play-world are thus established: a world of floating undead babies, 'horsed / Upon the sightless couriers of the air' (1.7.22–3), in which 'charnel-houses' and graves must send / Those that we bury back' (3.4.70–71), and where the 'poor country' of Scotland 'cannot / Be called our mother, but our grave' (4.3.165–7).

Clearly the Captain here wishes to say something different. He wants to evoke the idea of redemptive battle, or birth from death. But he cannot quite finish the thought: 'But I am faint. My gashes cry for help' (1.2.42). He means that his wounds ache and need treatment. But the personification suggests something much more uncanny. It suggests a gash with a tongue, crying out in pain, a cry

Placebo.

ilexi quoniam
exaudiet do
minus voce
orationis mee

uia inclinauit au
rem suam michi et in

Ce sera moy

Esse bonum didici quando: ne finge timorem
Hunc mihi: neu socijs curas iniunge molestas
Sic ait. obscurisq; fremens se condidit umbris
Nocte fere media cererem sumpsere per herbas
Effusi nudes celte. pars cetera seruat
Excubias: alij somno dant membra fluenti

ostera frugiferis reuehebat Lumina terris——

Aurora : & roseo Lustrauerat aethera curru

Nec minus ausonidum ductor fortissimus arma

Induit : irarumq; animis permittit habenas

Comparat haud natum genitori ipm q; uidere

Iam pherinanta cupit : uictum quem concipit iri

that resonates beyond the words that the captain actually speaks. Every wound in the field might be imagined weeping and wailing; the soundtrack of this world, its aural environment, comes from the dying and the dead.

The ubiquity of death and the dead is a material fact. But it is also a cue for any number of metaphors of death. Here is the neatly named Posthumus in *Cymbeline*, searching for death on a battlefield filled with the dead and dying:

> I, in mine own woe charmed,
> Could not find death where I did hear him groan,
> Nor feel him where he struck. Being an ugly monster,
> 'Tis strange he hides him in fresh cups, soft beds,
> Sweet words, or hath more ministers than we
> That draw his knives i'th' war. Well, I will find him.
>
> (5.5.68–73)

As with Hamlet, there is a horrible identification here of death with beauty and seductiveness: not only the thought that you might be mugged as you sleep or kiss, but that these things are in themselves foretastes and 'ministers' of death, or death in disguise, drawing you into your fated end, turning all of life into a dance with death.

Places such as Posthumus's battlefield are the reverse of the traditional pastoral garden, where death is waylaid and fertility eternal. But in fact even Shakespeare's apparently more conventional pastoral worlds can be supercharged with death. Recall Adonis in Shakespeare's poem, killed by a boar; or the stricken deer in *As You Like It*, moralized by the melancholy Jaques into a symbol of 'country, city, court, / Yea, and of this our life' (2.1.59–60). The Lords would mock Jaques for his 'sullen' sentiment, but Shakespeare gives so many words to the deer's dying that it takes on its own unsettling, durable reality:

> To the which place a poor sequestered stag
> That from the hunter's aim had ta'en a hurt
> Did come to languish. And indeed my lord,

Figure 52 *previous page* Later damage to this delicate fifteenth-century Italian illumination of battle overlays its bright, distinct colours with something darker and more chaotic, something akin to the way the soldiers before Agincourt in *Henry V* undercut the pomp and heraldry with their fear of the judgement that awaits them. Basinio de' Basini, *Hesperides*, an epic praising the campaigns of Sigismondo Malatesta (Rimini 1457–68): Bodleian Library, MS. Canon. Class. Lat. 81, fol. 122v.

The wretched animal heaved forth such groans
That their discharge did stretch his leathern coat
Almost to bursting, and the big round tears
Coursed one another down his innocent nose
In piteous chase.

(2.1.33–40)

The sporting 'chase' of the hunters gives way to the 'piteous chase' of the deer's tears as it slowly watches itself die:

… thus the hairy fool,
Much markèd of the melancholy Jaques,
Stood on th'extremest verge of the swift brook,
Augmenting it with tears.

(40–43)

In some ways Shakespeare is laying it on thick here: Jaques would turn the deer into a pathetic metaphor of his own exquisite misery; all the others look forward to the deer bleeding to death and in due course being served up for dinner. But still this killing represents an invasion of something sacrosanct:

… we
Are mere usurpers, tyrants, and what's worse,
To fright the animals and to kill them up
In their assigned and native dwelling-place.

(2.1.60–63)

Enjoy your feast, just as you enjoy your comedy; but don't forget that leisure, like all power, exacts its cost.

The deer is a good example of Shakespeare's unsleeping feeling for the life in anything, human or not. As Hamlet puts it, 'There's a special providence in the fall of a sparrow' (5.2.65–6). It is the basic principle of Shakespearean death – the

'providence' being not so much of God, but of the play-world's directing purposes, in which each death expresses life.

In Shakespeare's sweepingly intimate imagination, anything might be alive – which means that anything might die, or experience the fear of doing so. This helps explain how Shakespeare's metaphors often seem to tremble with life and feeling; and why they can so effortlessly express the pathos of mortality:

> Before the sun rose he was harnessed light,
> And to the field goes he, where every flower
> Did as a prophet weep what it foresaw
> In Hector's wrath.
>
> (*Troilus and Cressida*, 1.2.8–11)

The great Trojan warrior Hector, 'harnessed' for battle, is imagined here as a wrathful mower, preparing to level the field in anger. It is early in the morning and the flowers are wet with dew. The dew becomes the tears of the flowers, weeping for their own imminent destruction, which also foretells the numberless victims of the battle about to recommence. Death is no longer something distant, no longer a statistic: 'every flower' is weeping.

Shakespeare's tragedies are grounded still more deeply in this kinship of place and death. Again, Hamlet's graveyard is a touchstone. For remember: this scene is also Hamlet's homecoming. He returns from his madness and wildness precisely to a yard of graves, the childhood home that has patiently been awaiting.

Romeo and Juliet is headed throughout to its climax in the tomb. Juliet will have Romeo, whatever the consequences. She breaks gradually away from all the false, constricting places of daily life – streets, gardens, ballrooms, even bedrooms – and moves into places that better express the death-risking ultimacy of her desire:

> Chain me with roaring bears,
> Or hide me nightly in a charnel-house,

Figure 53 The deathbed, pictured here in a Book of Hours, was a common motif on stage – most ominously at the end of Othello. Death of the Virgin Mary, from the Hours of Engelbert of Nassau (Flemish, 1470s), Bodleian Library, MSS. Douce 219–220, fol. 170v.

O'ercovered quite with dead men's rattling bones,
With reeky shanks and yellow chapless skulls;
Or bid me go into a new-made grave,
And hide me with a dead man in his shroud

(4.1.80–85)

In one sense Juliet is evoking the foulest, most alien thing she can possibly imagine. She would endure this ignominy and disgust rather than forsake her lover. But at the same time Juliet is remaking herself as a creature that most truly belongs elsewhere than daylight and daylife. In being covered by the rattling bones of the dead, or nestled beneath a shroud with a corpse, she is imagining a metabolic alteration, a refitting of her own bones with those of the dead.

As always in Shakespeare, language has a magical capacity to come true, to predict the future, to evoke possibilities that are more real than the paltry state of things that can be seen with our eyes. So it is here: the 'new-made grave' she projects herself into will be her own; it *is* her own.

In due course the plot fulfils what the language here foreshadows. Juliet drinks the sleeping potion, she is thought dead by all who love her, and she comes back to life in a tomb. Finally, inevitably, Romeo discovers her in the tomb, in the 'palace of dim light', attended by 'worms that are thy chambermaids'. When she wakes and sees Romeo's dead body, there is nothing left to do but kiss his lips and stab herself with the 'happy dagger'. But the tomb is more than a setting for catastrophe. It is the physical manifestation of that catastrophe, and of the desires that made it unavoidable. Place expresses the tragedy quite as much as do the characters – the tragedy being that this hideous, bone-riddled tomb is the only answer and habitat for their 'death-marked love' (Prologue, 9). No wonder Romeo calls it a 'womb of death' (5.3.45).

The most powerful expression of this teasing with death is another speech of Juliet's that envisions rather than actually experiences what it will be like to awaken with the dead:

>   ... is it not like that I
> So early waking – what with loathsome smells,
> And shrieks like mandrakes torn out of the earth,
> That living mortals, hearing them, run mad –
> Or if I wake, shall I not be distraught,
> Environèd with all these hideous fears,
> And madly play with my forefathers' joints,
> And pluck the mangled Tybalt from his shroud,
> And, in this rage, with some great kinsman's bone
> As with a club dash out my desp'rate brains?
>
>   (4.3.44–53)

Juliet speaks here of 'living mortals' as though they are another species – or rather a species that she in her 'madness' must leave behind. In part she shall leave it behind because she will kill herself – that fact is already clear. More profoundly, 'living mortals' have become alien to Juliet because she is *already* one with the dead and with things immortal. The mythical afterlife of Juliet is inextricable from her knowledge that life – living, breathing life – cannot cope with her desire. Death creates the life of Romeo and Juliet.

All of Shakespeare's tragedies happen in – even happen *as* – environments that in themselves suggest a vision of death. Sometimes this place is a luxurious deathbed, as in Cleopatra's pillowed departure, or the marital bed that is the focus of all eyes and the site of murder in *Othello*. Sometimes the place is bare, wild, stripped of comfort, such that the terrain seems itself to suffer in death, being punished, remorseless, inescapable and frigid. And in this very implacability, in the fact that it can never alter, the place dwarfs the single human, reducing them to powerlessness, to a tiny cry in the wind, just as death does: 'Tom's a-cold!' (*King Lear*, 3.2.55).

The greatest example of this is probably *King Lear*. The play begins with Lear dividing up his kingdom and conferring his land and power 'on younger strengths, while we / Unburdened crawl toward death' (1.1. 40–41). From the start we can understand Lear's movements as a death crawl, with Lear at the very verge of existing and not. Lear's journey passes from the known living world into an alienated wilderness, a limbo in which the boundary of life and death is forever in doubt. The pivotal scene is when Lear realizes that he will find no home with any of his children. He has already banished Cordelia, and now he discovers that neither Goneril nor Regan will endure his retinue. He wants a hundred knights, which number is halved, and halved again, reduced to ten, then five, and then, with terminal finality, to none at all: 'What need one?' (2.2.437). The knights are more than the vestiges of Lear's authority. To strip them is to strip him, unit by unit, of his very substance. In one sense he is left alone with himself, in existential isolation. But in a deeper sense he is reduced to nothing, because all that identified him is lost. If he isn't a dead man already, he is left alone to face his death.

The model for the great scene in which Lear is abandoned to the storm is the early-sixteenth-century morality play *Everyman*. This play is about the 'art of dying'. The titular character is summoned by Death but resists the summons because he is unready. He wants to tarry a little. When Death insists, Everyman tries to persuade others to join him in his trip. He meets with Fellowship, Kindred and Cousin, but one after the other, for all their protestations of love and care, they declare that they will not accompany him: 'As for me, ye shall go alone' (354). Everyman must travel solitary into death. The same happens to Lear through the scenes in the storm, in the hovel, and in the wastes near Dover. He enters the fringes of death, and must come to terms with a life almost over. This is why in the storm scenes the only interlocutors Lear recognizes are the gods, the weather, or Poor Tom – a chattering, skeletal 'spirit', re-suffering all of his crimes, possessed by demons, a figure seemingly straight from the pains of limbo. Each 'station' on Lear's journey is a pathetic fallacy of death: a thunderous catastrophe, purgatorial torture, living burial, surreal judgement, a dizzying cliff, a wild heath, a sulphurous pit, a wheel of fire.

It can be no surprise that when he wakes from his journey and sees his ministering spirit (in fact his daughter Cordelia), Lear very simply believes that he has been and remains in death:

Lear	You do me wrong to take me out o'th' grave.
	Thou art a soul in bliss, but I am bound
	Upon a wheel of fire, that mine own tears
	Do scald like molten lead.
Cordelia	Sir, do you know me?
Lear	You are a spirit, I know. Where did you die?

(4.6.38–42)

This is not mere delusion. It really is what the play is having him experience. It is the strange audacity of works like *Lear* to imaginatively enter death, and emerge precariously at the other end.

A different take on the landscape of death is found in *Timon of Athens*. In exiling himself from Athens, Timon has banished himself not only from society and fellowship, but from active life. He prays for disease and death to eat up communities, and he wilfully seeks out a landscape that might reflect back his own desolation: one of 'bleak air', 'cold brook', 'bare unhousèd trunks' and the 'conflicting elements exposed' (4.3.223–31). Timon reduces nature to a killing parody of nurture:

I have a tree which grows here in my close
That mine own use invites me to cut down,
And shortly I must fell it. Tell my friends …
From high to low throughout, that whoso please
To stop affliction, let him take his haste,
Come hither ere my tree hath felt the axe,
And hang himself.

(5.2.90–97)

The tree is to all intents the last tree on earth. It is about to be cut down, but for as long as it stands it can serve as the gallows for all the world's sufferers. The natural world is shrunk into death's accessory. The roots he vows to live on are not the beginning of trees, but their end, the final tendrils of life to gnaw on before death. Timon's anti-pilgrimage is preparing for its ultimate resting place:

> Come not to me again, but say to Athens,
> Timon hath made his everlasting mansion
> Upon the beachèd verge of the salt flood,
> Who once a day with his embossèd froth
> The turbulent surge shall cover.
>
> (99–103)

Shakespeare is punning here on the theatrical meaning of 'mansion': this death place isn't just Timon's eternal dwelling; it is the ultimate 'station' of the play, the location that banishes all others and distils all of the action. This is why Shakespeare twice repeats the image. First he does so prospectively:

> ... Timon, presently prepare thy grave;
> Lie where the light foam of the sea may beat
> Thy gravestone daily.
>
> (4.3.380–82)

And then after it has been achieved:

> My noble general, Timon is dead,
> Entombed upon the very hem o'th' sea
>
> (5.5.66–7)

Clearly the image is foundational: burial at the very cusp, neither land nor sea, an embattled verge marked by constant attrition, by never-ending wear and tear. The tomb is marked more by violence than peace, its stony immobility outdone and worn down by the still more eternal 'surge' of the tides. Instead of rest, there is the roaring, turbulent 'beat' of oblivion.

Here is an ultimate example of something Shakespeare often works at in his tragedies – the merging of person and place, such that the place itself expresses a life that finds its apotheosis in death. Notice how the phrases that ostensibly describe the tides – 'the salt flood', 'his embossed froth', 'the turbulent surge' –

Figure 54 A beautifully illuminated early sixteenth-century French Book of Hours shows a soul trapped in a monster's jaw and tormented by demons, accompanying the text of the Office of the Dead. Bodleian Library, MS. Rawl. liturg. e. 36, fol. 91r.

an Placebo
Ilea quonia
exaudiet do
mmus voce
ordinis mee
Quia incli
nauit aurem suam michi
et in diebus meis inuocabo
Circuundederunt me dolo
res mortis et pericula insfer
ni inuenerunt me
tribulationem et dolo-
rem et nomen domini
inuocaui
Domine libera animam
meam misericors dominus
et iustus et deus nr misert
Custodiens paruulos do
mmus humiliatus sum:
et liberauit me
Convertere anima mea

apply just as much to the unrepealable rage of Timon. This effect is underscored by the ambiguity of the pronouns, which can denote either sea or Timon. Similarly, the tomb itself is both static and moving – 'upon the very hem o'th' sea', like a wavering skirt – just as his corpse is both beached and flooded. Timon's life survives into his death. Or, rather, life and death collapse into each other, levelling purpose and significance. This life-in-death endures as constitutional entropy – revealed here as the basic condition of all matter. As Timon darkly puts it, 'nothing brings me all things' (5.2.73).

When the human can so absolutely be compounded with the mute, unfeeling elements – and when this barren fate is celebrated as necessary and fitting poetic justice – life really has come to nothing:

> The enemy's drum is heard, and fearful scouring
> Doth choke the air with dust.
>
> (5.3.15–16)

8

DIE, DIE, DIE, DIE, DIE:

Cueing Death

Death on stage is different from death offstage. It is scripted, so that the person doing the dying knows in advance when and how. And it is performed by an actor, whose professional craft helps to ensure that the event gives the satisfactions that it should, whether vengeful, poignant, disturbing or even funny.

The extraordinary care that Shakespeare takes in scripting death scenes is founded in the parts he wrote for actors, and the very specific way in which these roles were transcribed, distributed, learnt, rehearsed, and then performed. The actors didn't get a copy of the playbook (there was usually only one). They received only their own part (or parts), a sheet or roll listing in due order their entrance and speech cues (usually between one and three words) and their speeches. The speaker of the cue was not named; nor was any information given about the time lapse between any two speeches. The individual part was thus given its own gap-ridden integrity – separated from others, at once self-complete and radically inadequate.

We might think that rehearsal would resolve any difficulties, telling the actor exactly how his part fitted in with others. But rehearsal didn't work in the same way as it does today. There would usually be one read-through, and some complicated ensemble scenes might be rehearsed once. But individual parts would overwhelmingly be learnt and practised alone (or occasionally in pairs), such

Burly house   Harowe on the hill

Durham house   Iuy lane   Bedford house   Sauoy   Somerset house   Arondell house   Esex staires   Whitefryers staires   Bridwell staires   Blackfryers staires

The Swan

S. PAULES CHURCH

Hamsted Mills

the Water
house

Hamsted

S. Brides

Castle

Pauls Wharfe

Quene Hythe

Three Cranes

The S

The Eell Schipes

The Gally fuste

THAMESIS

The Bear Gardne

The Globe

that the player would have to guess at the specific context or take on trust the movement and motives of his fellow participants. What is more, the player would often be acting multiple parts in a single week (there was rarely any guarantee of a second performance).

The consequence of this system of writing and learning parts is obvious. When it came to acting their parts in performance, the player would have to be on his toes, nervously alert to the unfolding action. He would have to adapt to surprise, interruption or unexpected delay. But as much as he might often have to improvise the timing and tenor of his responses, one thing remained sacrosanct: his own part and his own cues, from which he must not depart, and in which he must place faith as in his very existence.

In this system, moment-by-moment scripting was everything. There were no modern-style directors. The part alone had to direct the action. But luckily Shakespeare could rely – like no other writer could – upon the technical knowledge and professional experience of his actors. For, unique among playwrights, through-out his career Shakespeare was able to write his parts for the same core group of players. They developed their crafts together – and among them a new way of orchestrating on-stage deaths.

Dying on stage can be a difficult trick to pull off, with the danger of stretching the act to absurdity, or rendering the action static and bathetic as everyone stops and watches until the departing figure gasps their last. But it was an essential trick for the English popular stage to learn. After all, one of the chief differences between the Elizabethan and earlier drama – classical and vernacular – was that death was no longer merely a reported or anticipated event. It was actually enacted before the spectator's eyes. If it didn't come off then the whole play was liable to seem foolish and fake.

The particular trick that Shakespeare and his company discovered was the dying cue – or, more particularly, a *repeated dying cue*.

An actor always has to wait for his cue before speaking. Equally, the speaking actor knows that until he says his cue, he will not be interrupted. But what

Figure 55 *previous page* Engraved in the year of Shakespeare's death, this London panorama shows the playhouses of the Bankside at the bottom, and the dominant city church of St Paul's at the top – but the large expanse of empty sky suggests some more cosmic framing for everyday life along the Thames thoroughfare. Claes Janszoon Visscher's London, 1616. Bodleian Library, Douce Prints a.53 (2).

Figure 56 The actors of the Chamberlain's, later the King's Men, including the tragic star Richard Burbage, as listed in the 1623 First Folio. Bodleian Library, Arch. G c.7.

The Workes of William Shakespeare,

containing all his Comedies, Histories, and Tragedies: Truely set forth, according to their first ORJGJNALL.

The Names of the Principall Actors
in all these Playes.

Lliam Shakespeare.

Richard Burbadge.

John Hemmings.

Augustine Phillips.

William Kempt.

Thomas Poope.

George Bryan.

Henry Condell.

William Slye.

Richard Cowly.

John Lowine.

Samuell Crosse.

Alexander Cooke.

Samuel Gilburne.

Robert Armin.

William Ostler.

Nathan Field.

John Underwood.

Nicholas Tooley.

William Ecclestone.

Joseph Taylor.

Robert Benfield.

Robert Goughe.

Richard Robinson.

Iohn Shancke.

Iohn Rice.

Enter Richard.

Rich. A Horse, a Horse, my Kingdome for a Horse.
Cates. Withdraw my Lord, Ile helpe you to a Horse
Rich. Slaue, I haue set my life vpon a cast,
And I will stand the hazard of the Dye:
I thinke there be sixe Richmonds in the field,
Fiue haue I slaine to day, in stead of him.
A Horse, a Horse, my Kingdome for a Horse.

Alarum, Enter Richard and Richmond, they fight, Richard is slaine.

Retreat, and Flourish. Enter Richmond, Derby bearing the Crowne, with diuers other Lords.

Richm. God, and your Armes
Be prais'd Victorious Friends;
The day is ours, the bloudy Dogge is dead.
Der. Couragious Richmond,
Well hast thou acquit thee: Loe,
Heere these long vsurped Royalties,
From the dead Temples of this bloudy Wretch,
Haue I pluck'd off, to grace thy Browes withall.
We are it, and make much of it.
Richm. Great God of Heauen, say Amen to all:
But tell me, is yong George Stanley liuing?
Der. He is my Lord, and safe in Leicester Towne,
Whither (if you please) we may withdraw vs.
Richm. What men of name are slaine on either side?

Der. John Duke of Norfolke, Walter Lord Ferris,
Sir Robert Brokenbury, and Sir William Brandon.
Richm. Interre their Bodies, as become their Birth,
Proclaime a pardon to the Soldiers fled,
That in submission will returne to vs,
And then as we haue tane the Sacrament,
We will vnite the White Rose, and the Red.
Smile Heauen vpon this faire Coniunction,
That long haue frown'd vpon their Enmity:
What Traitor heares me, and sayes not Amen?
England hath long beene mad, and scar'd her selfe;
The Brother blindely shed the Brothers blood;
The Father, rashly slaughtered his owne Sonne;
The Sonne compell'd, beene Butcher to the Sire;
All this diuided Yorke and Lancaster,
Diuided, in their dire Diuision,
O now, let Richmond and Elizabeth,
The true Succeeders of each Royall House,
By Gods faire ordinance, conioyne together:
And let thy Heires (God if thy will be so)
Enrich the time to come, with Smooth-fac'd Peace,
With smiling Plenty, and faire Prosperous dayes.
Abate the edge of Traitors, Gracious Lord,
That would reduce these bloudy dayes againe,
And make poore England weepe in Streames of Blood;
Let them not liue to taste this Lands increase,
That would with Treason, wound this faire Lands peace.
Now Ciuill wounds are stopp'd, Peace liues agen;
That she may long liue heere, God say, Amen. *Exeunt*

FINIS.

The Famous History of the Life of King HENRY the Eight.

THE PROLOGUE.

I Come no more to make you laugh, Things now,
That beare a Weighty, and a Serious Brow,
Sad, high, and working, full of State and Woe:
Such Noble Scaenes, as draw the Eye to flow
We now present. Those that can Pitty, heere
May (if they thinke it well) let fall a Teare,
The Subiect will deserue it. Such as giue
Their Money out of hope they may beleeue,
May heere finde Truth too. Those that come to see
Onely a show or two, and so agree
The Play may passe: If they be still, and willing,
Ile vndertake may see away their shilling
Richly in two short houres. Onely they
That come to heare a Merry, Bawdy Play,
A noyse of Targets: Or to see a Fellow
In a long Motley Coate, garded with Yellow,
Will be deceyu'd. For gentle Hearers, know
To ranke our chosen Truth with such a show
As Foole, and Fight is, beside forfeiting
Our owne Braines, and the Opinion that we bring
To make that onely true, we now intend,
Will leaue vs neuer an vnderstanding Friend;
Therefore, for Goodnesse sake, and as you are know
The First and Happiest Hearers of the Towne,
Be sad, as we would make ye. Thinke ye see
The very Persons of our Noble Story,
As they were Liuing: Thinke you see them Great,
And follow'd with the generall throng, and sweat
Of thousand Friends: Then, in a moment, see
How soone this Mightinesse, meets Misery:
And if you can be merry then, Ile say,
A Man may weepe vpon his Wedding day.

Actus Primus. Scœna Prima.

Enter the Duke of Norfolke at one doore. At the other, the Duke of Buckingham, and the Lord Abergauenny.

Buckingham.
Good morrow, and well met. How haue ye done
Since last we saw in France?
Norf. I thanke your Grace:
Healthfull, and euer since a fresh Admirer
Of what I saw there.
Buck. An vntimely Ague
Staid me a Prisoner in my Chamber, when
Those Sunnes of Glory, those two Lights of Men
Met in the vale of Andren.
Nor. Twixt Guynes and Arde,
I was then present, saw them salute on Horsebacke,
Beheld them when they lighted, how they clung
In their Embracement, as they grew together,
Which had they,
What foure Thron'd ones could haue weigh'd
Such a compounded one?
Buck. All the whole time
I was my Chambers Prisoner.

Nor. Then you lost
The view of earthly glory: Men might say
Till this time Pompe was single, but now married
To one aboue it selfe. Each following day
Became the next dayes master, till the last
Made former Wonders, it's. To day the French,
All Clinquant all in Gold, like Heathen Gods
Shone downe the English; and to morrow, they
Made Britaine, India: Euery man that stood,
Shew'd like a Mine. Their Dwarfish Pages were
As Cherubins, all gilt: the Madams too,
Not vs'd to toyle, did almost sweat to beare
The Pride vpon them, that their very labour
Was to them, as a Painting. Now this Maske
Was cry'de incomparable; and th'ensuing night
Made it a Foole, and Begger. The two Kings
Equall in lustre, were now best, now worst
As presence did present them: Him in eye,
Still him in praise, and being present both,
'Twas said they saw but one, and no Discerner
Durst wagge his Tongue in censure, when these Sunnes
(For so they phrase 'em) by their Heralds challeng'd
The Noble Spirits to Armes, they did performe

t 3	B

happens if the cue is spoken twice? When exactly will the cued response come in? Let us look at some examples.

Here are the famous last words of Richard III: 'A horse! A horse! My kingdom for a horse!' (5.7.7) at which point the Folio text adds the following stage directions: 'Alarum. Enter King Richard and Henry Earl of Richmond. They fight. Richard is slain.' (Figure 57). Modern editions and performances usually make Richard exit after speaking this line, and then reappear on stage fighting. But notice how the line is scripted. The cue 'a horse' appears not once, but three times. And so when exactly does Richard exit, or the alarum sound, or Richmond enter, or their fight begin? When exactly is Richard slain? And when exactly does he die?

We have to remember here that the cue words appear on at least two parts: the part of the speaker, and the part of the actors cued. In the event of a repeated cue, this gives unique theatrical power to the speaker. He will see that his cue comes before his speech has ended. This means that if he wishes he can 'cue' his fellow players with the first articulation of the cue phrase – leaving the rest of his speech in his own possession, to be spoken whenever he chooses in the gaps or remissions of the action. In the case of Richard's final words, the actor could pause after saying 'A horse!', allow the alarum to be sounded, bring on Richmond (and perhaps other soldiers), and still have another 'A horse!', and 'My kingdom for a horse!', to say. His desperation can be amplified as the scene extends, with Richmond all the time closing in on his prey. The repeated cue, in other words, gives space for the acting of the death scene.

Now we might think it unlikely that Richard would pause in the middle of this famous line (although it wasn't famous when Burbage first played it). The pentameter is so sonorous and ringing it must be cried out as one. But what, then, to make of the fact that Richard says the complete line – his final line, his dying words – not once, but twice? Here is the scene in full from Richard's entrance to his death:

Enter King Richard
King Richard   A horse! A horse! My kingdom for a horse!

Figure 57. The final page of *Richard III* from the 1623 Folio shows the triumph of history – his nemesis, Richmond – and the famous line 'A horse! A horse! My kingdom for a horse'.

Catesby	Withdraw, my Lord. I'll help you to a horse.
King Richard	Slave, I have set my life upon a cast,
	And I will stand the hazard of the die.
	I think there be six Richmonds in the field.
	Five have I slain today, instead of him.
	A horse! A horse! My kingdom for a horse!

Alarum. Enter King Richard and Henry Earl of Richmond. They fight. Richard is slain.

(5.7.7–13)

If the cue for Richmond is 'a horse', then it is spoken no fewer than six times. Even if Richmond's cue was the memorable 'My kingdom for a horse!', then it is spoken twice. It seems clear that Richmond is cued to enter before Richard stops speaking, and that the Richard actor is therefore liberated to act his dying exactly as he thinks right, feeling the moment, 'cued' only by his own discretion. It is even possible that his final line, or part of it, is spoken alone, *after* he has been slain. Modern editions like to insert a stage direction at this moment: '*Richard's body is carried off*'. But there is no such instruction in the original. Perhaps Richmond delivers the blow and exits, leaving Richard briefly alone on the stage with his pitiable, lonely valediction still to speak:

My kingdom for a horse

In a moment Richmond will re-enter with a victorious '*flourish*'. But Richard and his actor – appropriate to the terminal moment – get to do their dying alone.

A similar example is the killing of Mercutio in *Romeo and Juliet* – often thought to be the decisive moment in the plot, when a would-be romantic comedy suddenly turns tragic:

Mercutio	Help me into some house, Benvolio,
	Or I shall faint. A plague o' both your houses.
	They have made worms' meat of me.
	I have it, and soundly, too. Your houses! *Exit*

Romeo	This gentleman, the Prince's near ally,
	My very friend, hath got his mortal hurt
	In my behalf, my reputation stained
	With Tybalt's slander – Tybalt, that an hour
	Hath been my cousin! O sweet Juliet,
	Thy beauty hath made me effeminate,
	And in my temper softened valour's steel.
Enter Benvolio	
Benvolio	O Romeo, Romeo, brave Mercutio is dead!
	(3.1.105–16)

In performance this is usually played in the simple order in which it seems to be written: Mercutio is bleeding to death; he curses the houses; he is carried offstage; Romeo is left alone to speak his soliloquy, expressing his guilt and shame; and then Benvolio re-enters to confirm that Mercutio has died. But if we pay attention to the cues we can see an alternative way of staging death. Mercutio speaks his departing cue ('your houses') twice; indeed in the first Quarto edition of the play from 1597 he speaks it four times, with a slight variation: 'A pox o' your houses!' What this means is that Romeo can start his speech of self-rebuke while the Mercutio actor still has things to say in the intervals of Romeo's 'soliloquy':

They have made worms' meat of me.
I have it, and soundly, too. Your houses!

It makes perfect dramatic sense: Romeo initially seems to be speaking about someone present on the stage ('this gentleman'), to whom he feels and addresses great affection ('My very friend'). Meanwhile Mercutio is in his own head, isolated and hopeless, bleeding to death.

The cueing technique allows him to pass away at his own pace, in his own space, even as people are swarming around him. It is a simple technique, allowing for both dramatic verisimilitude and psychological intimacy. It avoids static, artificial, procedural successiveness, in which one figure speaks, then dies, others pause and watch, only resuming their speaking once the final words are done and death has arrived. It dramatizes instead the fact of different minds and bodies acting simultaneously. They can be at once coordinate, responding to the same terrible event, and in their own unreachably selfish worlds. Death is witnessed by many, but experienced alone.

Ironically, it is perhaps the funniest death in all of the plays that reveals the full potentiality of this technique – Bottom's performance of Pyramus's suicide in *A Midsummer Night's Dream*:

> Out sword, and wound
> The pap of Pyramus.
> Ay, that left pap,
> Where heart doth hop;
> Thus die I: thus, thus, thus.
> Now am I dead,
> Now am I fled,
> My soul is in the sky.
> Tongue lose thy light;
> Moon take thy flight,
> Now die, die, die, die, die.

Demetrius	No die but an ace for him; for he is but one.
Lysander	Less than an ace, man; for he is dead; he is nothing.
Theseus	With the help of a surgeon he might yet recover and prove an ass.

(5.1.291–306)

Shakespeare is both parodying and extending his own techniques. Consider the doubled-up repetitive phrases in Pyramus's dying words: first 'thus, thus, thus', then 'die, die, die, die, die'. The first one, it seems, should mark Pyramus' passing away; with the final 'thus' he is dead. After 'Pyramus' dies, Bottom reverts to himself, as actor, and explains what his character is even *now* experiencing: 'Now am I dead, / Now am I fled, / My soul is in the sky.' He is imagining his character traversing the lands beyond the temporal. But then Bottom is so transported by this vision that he re-enters his 'character' – who therefore has to die all over again (and again, and again).

Clearly the scene is mocking stage deaths – their excruciating elongation, the egotism of the actor who will not go quietly, the self-evident falsity and absurdity of the whole charade. More specifically Shakespeare is either burlesquing or preparing for the death scenes in *Romeo and Juliet* – both the lovers' and Mercutio's, whose 'gallant spirit hath aspired the clouds', and whose 'soul' when dead is reported 'but a little way above our heads' (3.1.117, 126–7), a pathetic echo of Bottom's bathetic 'Now am I fled … / My soul is in the sky'.

Shakespeare is exposing his own machinery, the basic facts of theatre that must frame and mediate any acting of death: that an actor speaks from a pre-written script, from which he does not (or should not) depart; that the character dies, but the actor does not; that the actor can have perspective upon the character, can 'watch' him pass away, comment upon it after it has seemed to happen, or as he is playing dead; that what we witness is the idea of death, its simulacrum, and never anything more; that no one can quite die on stage.

But even as this machinery is here made very transparent, the scene exposes the potential of theatre to strangely enter and question the experience of dying. When exactly does Pyramus die? Does he die more than once? Does he die, return to life, die again, return again? Does he survive his own death? Or is he wrapped up in the singular process of *his* departure, oblivious to all interruptions, all laughter, entering his one and only death in the hallowed existential cocoon created by his repeated cues? Shakespeare here parodies – or perhaps discovers – what in later tragedies becomes the profoundest engagement with the shadowlands between living and death.

Repeated cues become the basic method through which Shakespeare orchestrates tragic departures. Whether spoken by the one entering death – Ophelia's 'Goodnight, goodnight', Lady Macbeth's 'To bed, to bed, to bed', Lear's 'Look there, look there' – or by the figures crowding in upon them – as happens with Brutus, Coriolanus and Claudius – the actor is allowed a sacred freedom in which to feel out and enact his character's disappearance. Even Hamlet's famous dying sentence – 'The rest is silence' – is succeeded in the Folio text by four repeating utterances:

O, o, o, o, *Dyes*.

As Horatio bids his 'sweet prince' goodnight, as the 'flights of angels' sing him to his rest (*Hamlet*, 5.2.12–13), the actor may still be moaning and the character still suffering, hearing his own obituary, witnessing the sadness of his passing, gripping to life as it ebbs resistlessly away.

Through scripting like this, Shakespeare allows his characters to enter a space *in-between* life and death, consciousness and oblivion. He manufactures a kind of imaginary posthumousness, a living-and-dying threshold, allowed by the fact that the actor and the part continue even though the plot says the character has gone.

In moments such as these, theatre intuits a rare privilege: a probationary entrance into experiences that real life can never report, never return from. All of Shakespeare's great central tragedies explore such possibilities. This is at the heart of the dizzying 'Dover cliff' scene in *King Lear*, when Edgar verbally paints a cliff from which his father then actually leaps. The Gloucester actor drops to the stage floor, and his character believes that he has fallen from a great height. The audience sees that Gloucester is deluded; the possibility of death on stage seems to be pre-empted by situational irony. But then his son, having manufactured the pantomime, momentarily fears that this fall has indeed resulted in death ('Alive or dead?'). He finds to his relief that his father still breathes, and proceeds to a marvelous lie about watching him 'perpendicularly fall', a plummet that can only have resulted in the old man being 'shivered like an egg' (4.5.45–54). The old man leaves the scene believing that his life is indeed a miracle, a return from certain death.

It is a fiction, but the description, like that of the cliff itself, is so vivid as to take on counterfactual reality. Suicide *was* enacted: and yet it didn't happen. We know with our empirical faith that it was no more than a trick. But this is to underestimate the spell of words in a play-world, and the fact that it is primarily language that engenders their virtual realities. Just as Gloucester saw in his mind's eye the cliff from which he jumped, we too have 'seen' the cliff verge, 'heard' the chafe of waves upon pebbles far below, 'felt' the heady temptation to 'Topple down headlong'. 'But have I fall'n, or no?' asks Gloucester, his senses deranged by phenomenal overflow (*King Lear*, 4.5.11–56). Has he? We might equally answer yes as no. In scenes such as these Shakespeare takes theatre's tempting with death, its rehearsal of death's possibility, to the very 'verge'.

One of the most probing death scenes is Desdemona's in *Othello*. It touches intimately upon processes that are at once symbiotic and radically existentially separate: the process of killing and the process of being killed; the process of living and the process of dying; the process of acting a murderer and the process of acting a murder victim; and the processes, different from all of these, of being dead and of acting dead.

As it happens this scene was the subject of one of the very few eyewitness reports of Shakespeare's company in action – the diplomat Henry Jackson's account of a 1610 performance in Oxford:

> Moreover that famous Desdemona killed before us by her husband, although she acted her whole part supremely well, yet *when she was killed* she was even more moving, for when she fell back upon the bed she implored the pity of the spectators by her very face.[29] [stress added]

The report was written in Latin, and its crucial word is *interfecta*. It is translated here as 'when she was killed', but can also mean 'in her death'. Jackson may be referring to her piteous face *once* she had been killed; he may be referring to her face *as* she was being killed. So in what state exactly – alive or dead – was her face as it 'implored the pity of the spectators'? Was it a direct appeal to appalled witnesses, or a stilled expression into which the spectator projected emotion? It is impossible to say – and this is exactly the point.

The ambiguity homes in upon the scene's decisive questions, for actor, character and audience. How to know whether Desdemona is living or dying or dead? And what does it mean to act such a thing – appealing to spectators, playing a part to the best of one's abilities – and yet also to *be* the face and body, or be identical to the face and body, that arouses emotion and experiences death?

The scene is unique in all sorts of ways. No other murder is dramatized in such excruciating, step-by-step detail; no other murder victim is made so prescient of what is happening, all the way through to the barely believable fact of its occurrence; no other murderer has to return, over and over, to his object, checking the efficiency of his methods, feeling his victim's life as it drips gradually away. And yet at the same time as this remorseless concentration upon the facts – *someone right now is killing, someone right here is being killed* – the scene also generates the most exquisite physical and metaphysical mysteries, as we try to peer into or guess at what exactly is happening.

First, there is Desdemona's moment-by-moment consciousness of what is about to happen: the awful awakening of recognition, her horror at the prospect of death, her desperate clinging to life, her sustained pleas of innocence, her protests trying to delay her lunatic husband's hand:

Talk you of killing? (5.2.35)
Then heaven / Have mercy on me. (35–6)
I hope you will not kill me. (37)
… but yet I feel I fear. (41)
I hope, I hope / They do not point on me. (48–9)
… not yet to die! (56)
Lord have mercy on me. (62)
I never did / Offend you in my life (63–4)
I never gave it him. (72)
Alas, he is betrayed, and I undone. (83)
O, banish me, my lord, but kill me not! (85)
Kill me tomorrow; let me live tonight. (87)
But half an hour! (89)
But while I say one prayer. (91)

Figure 58 Othello's agony here may be pre- or post- Desdemona's murder in the protracted scene in which death, acting, and voyeurism are all probed. From *A collection of prints, from pictures painted [for the Shakespeare gallery of John and Josiah Boydell]*, 1803. Bodleian Library, Johnson a.59 (v.2)

In all of Shakespeare there is no more sustained living in the imminence, terror and injustice of self-annihilation than this.

Second, there is the scene's insistence on the sheer physical exertion of murdering someone, both the malice aforethought and the technical attention to means and ends that it requires. Othello begins the act of killing with his dismissive 'It is too late', followed by the stage direction '*Smothers her*' ('*Stifles her*' in the Quarto text). The Desdemona part has no words during this process of killing (presumably her face is being smothered by the pillow or bolster). But the Othello part has a sequence of intra-speech cues, each one asking the actor to continue prodding, testing, pushing or pressing his fellow actor's body:

> Not dead? Not yet quite dead? …
> I would not have thee linger in thy pain, – so, so. …
>   … by and by: she's dead. …
> The noise was here
>
>   [Quarto]
>
> Ha! No more moving. …
> I think she stirs again. No. What's best to do? …
> Soft, by and by.
>
>   (5. 2.102–13)

This is no simple execution. The whole purport of the scene is the *difficulty* of killing; the struggle to effect another's exit; and the uncertainty as to whether it has in fact been done.

Third, there is the unique afterlife of Desdemona – or, rather, the continuing presence that she has after the character has appeared to die. Ironically, this continuing presence is initially created by her visual disappearance. Emilia is knocking madly at the door to get in. To hide the evidence of what he has done Othello draws closed the bed-curtains. Desdemona's body is thus hidden from view – but imperfectly hidden, such that her form *might* be descried through the curtains, or beneath them, or between their margins if the wind were to blow. We know the curtains must in due course be opened and their horror exposed. The closed curtains, then, do not equal closure; they are a question mark, awaiting revelation.

We know that behind the curtains is the Desdemona actor. But what about *Desdemona* – her mind, her soul, her longings? Is *she* there or not? One thing is clear: that the question 'dead or alive?' remains vitally in play even when her body is hidden. And yet still it is shocking, strangely weird and estranging, when from behind the curtains comes Desdemona's voice:

O, falsely, falsely murdered!

Initially we do not see her. We only hear these disembodied words. Much of the strangeness comes from the very real uncertainty about where the voice is coming from:

Emilia	O Lord, what cry is that?
Othello	That? What?
(5.2.126–8)	

The voice is disembodied; it seems to come from death. Is death speaking? Is death coming to life? Is it the voice of a ghost?

It is at this point that Emilia draws the curtains open and sees her lady on the bed:

Emilia	Sweet Desdemona, O sweet mistress, speak!
Desdemona	A guiltless death I die.
Emilia	O, who hath done this deed?
Desdemona	Nobody, I myself. Farewell.
	Commend me to my kind lord. O, farewell!
(131–4)	

A peine fut levé le corps
Ou du moins en sepulchre mis
Que lors le bruit par dehors
De deux hostz trespuissans & fors
Chascun paré de ses amys
Accident, le premier Je dys
Qui sur le reng se vint embastre
Honté & armé pour combatre.

And so Desdemona dies – dies, it is tempting to say, again.

This moment often causes disbelief or even laughter – how can she be strangled or suffocated, revive to speak, and then immediately die? It is absurd, or grossly sentimental, made worse by the fact that she dies upon a lie.

We might rationalize the physiological insult by assuming that she dies not from suffocation but from haemorrhage: but this is really beside the point. Shakespeare seems to want to place Desdemona, or for us to rediscover Desdemona, *inside* this liminal space between active living and stony death. She may have briefly revived from coma; she may be slowly dying and gasping her last; she may be a returning ghost; she may be speaking from death, actually from the afterlife, from a state of grace where the petty mistakes of life are pre-emptively forgiven. All of these are possible: enabled by the fact that this is a play-world, not reality.

And we can go still further: precisely because this is a play, it is still not certain that Desdemona has in fact spoken her last words. For she too dies upon a repeated cue: 'farewell'. Once she has said it the first time, the action that succeeds Desdemona – her life if not her part – has therefore been cued. The character has gone. But then she still has her final words to speak: 'Commend me to my kind Lord. O, farewell.' What can this mean? When does she say them? Who does she say them to? Must she say them? The decision is the actor's alone.

Shakespeare is working here at the curious double-mindedness of play-worlds. The dying is suffered by a character but acted by an actor. The character has one mind, the actor has another. And yet at some inescapable level they must share a body, even if the one's body is never quite the other's. One body passes, while the other body remains to imitate this passing. It is a strange kind of taking hostage. But as we see with the repeated cue, it isn't quite sufficient to say that the actor plays the character's death, and then it is done, the relation between actor and character over. He – of course Desdemona was written for a male actor – may still have words in his safe keeping; the part can secretly survive its own apparent death.

The part of Desdemona does not end with its final speech. The actor must remain on stage for another 250 lines – exposed to public view, pointed at, spoken

Figure 59 A *grisaille* painting of an allegorical combat from the mid-seventeenth century. Fresh memory and the Author watch the combat between Duke Charles of Burgundy (Charles the Bold) and Accident. Atropos, on platform, is judge. Olivier de la Marche, *Le chevalier délibéré*: Bodleian Library, MS. Douce 168, fols. 45v–46r.

about, prodded, fallen upon, embraced, kissed, covered by another actor playing dead – until finally, mercifully, the curtain is drawn closed one final time. The Desdemona actor must keep on acting, alert to the actions of his fellows, careful not to sigh or shift position, mentally alert, professionally attuned, no doubt physically uncomfortable. Again and again the Desdemona actor is asked to rediscover his character inside weird deathlike spaces – behind the curtains, or inside the bracket of repeated cues, or after his own written part has ended.

These are spaces in which the dramatic action is voided, and in which the actor's own role has fallen into abeyance. And yet they are also spaces from which, in this very absence, indeed because of this absence, the actor is called upon, forced to be alert and animate, forced to *act* even in stillness. And just as the actor survives the character, and just as the character survives to be played by another actor, so too the part survives to be read over and over, forward and backward, by still others. It is the most basic fact of play life. There is action inside apparent death; there is movement in stillness; and there is never either final rest or true silence.

9

KINDLE AGAIN:

Life in Death

The life in death takes changeable forms. Ghosts appear at various times in Shakespeare. In *Richard III* the ghosts of Prince Edward, Henry VI, Clarence, the two princes in the tower, and so on, enter the sleep of King Richard and his challenger Richmond (the future Henry VII), cursing one, blessing the other (5.5.100–130). In *Julius Caesar* the Ghost of Caesar appears in the troubled insomnia of Brutus, telling him they shall meet again at Philippi. In *Macbeth* the blood-bolted ghost of Banquo enters the feast and sits in Macbeth's place, shaking his gory locks at the usurper.

In each of these cases the ghost is principally a marker of the protagonist's guilt. It isn't so much the murdered who cannot rest in peace. It is the murderers. We may get some feeling of the loneliness of death, a condition of sleepless, homeless, monomaniacal wandering – but again these feelings belong mainly to the sinful soul of the living. The ghosts are less figures of the afterlife than projections of restless ambition or emotional desire. It is clinging to this world – hoping, longing, wishing, regretting – that conjures fearful visions of death.

Only one ghost in Shakespeare truly stalks the lands beyond the living. This is King Hamlet, walking the battlements through the frigid darkness of night. The ghost's appearance – especially to young Hamlet – brings into palpable question the limits of nature, consciousness and knowledge:

O answer me!
Let me not burst in ignorance, but tell
Why thy canonized bones, hearsèd in death,
Have burst their cerements, why the sepulchre
Wherein we saw thee quietly enurned
Hath oped his ponderous and marble jaws
To cast thee up again. What may this mean,
That thou, dead corpse, again in complete steel,
Revisitst thus the glimpses of the moon,
Making night hideous, and we fools of nature
So horridly to shake our disposition
With thoughts beyond the reaches of our souls?
Say, why is this? Wherefore? What should we do?

(*Hamlet*, 1.4.26–38)

As Hamlet grimly jokes upon first seeing the apparition, 'Thou com'st in such a questionable shape / That I will speak to thee' (1.4.24–5). The shape is not only baffling – what is it? where does it come from? why is it here? – but dubious in its very being. Is it even here? Is it what it seems? And if it is, what does this mean about all that we thought we knew? When the grave seems to open, when the wastes of limbo are somehow *here* – then everything is suddenly 'questionable'. The visible world may be no more than a carapace over an abyss, or a sick membrane covering infinite corruption and punishment. It is the Ghost that tears opens the world of Hamlet, stretching the bounds of nature and the knowable (Figure 61).

And yet, as much as the Ghost reports suffering the fires of purgatory, 'Till the foul crimes done in my days of nature / Are burnt and purg'd away', the world beyond death remains shrouded:

But that I am forbid
To tell the secrets of my prison-house
I could a tale unfold whose lightest word
Would harrow up thy soul, freeze thy young blood,

Figure 60 Children are not safe in Shakespeare's plays: this early nineteenth-century print of the princes in the tower – a scene described by Shakespeare rather than shown – participates in something of the same queasy enjoyment of child-murder as plays including *Macbeth* and *King John*. Engraving after James Northcote, from *A collection of prints, from pictures painted [for the Shakespeare gallery of John and Josiah Boydell]*, 1803. (v.2), Bodleian Library, Johnson a.59.

Make thy two eyes like stars start from their spheres ...
But this eternal blazon must not be
To ears of flesh and blood.

(1.5.12–22)

The Ghost is doomed to walk in unquiet vexation (1.5.10–13), cursing the fact that his life was taken 'even in the blossoms' of his sin, all his 'imperfections' still on his head: 'O horrible, O horrible, most horrible!' (76–80). The worst of purgatory, it seems, is that life's emotions cannot be left behind. The Ghost dwells on his fleshly sins, on the crime of his murder, and on the continuing scandal of the royal bed, now a 'couch for luxury and damnèd incest' (83). He burns with the vices of living passion; indeed the Ghost is as fleshly a creature as Shakespeare ever made.

His call for revenge is the call of unsleeping life. As ever in Shakespeare, the horror of death is that life will not leave well enough alone. 'Rest, rest, perturbèd spirit', says Hamlet to the 'old mole' Ghost, but it is a vain imprecation (1.5.183, 164). In Shakespeare the afterlife cannot be thought of free from the things that it leaves behind. Desire stings even beyond the end.

Another figure in *Hamlet* who haunts beyond her life is Ophelia. She is reported drowned, and the Queen re-creates the memorable scene:

There is a willow grows aslant the brook
That shows his hoar leaves in the glassy stream.
Therewith fantastic garlands did she make
Of crow-flowers, nettles, daisies, and long purples,
That liberal shepherds give a grosser name,
But our cold maids do dead men's fingers call them.

(4.7.138–43)

The 'weedy trophies' she makes from the flowers will be her burial wreaths, compounded of the innocence of the daisy, the sting of the 'nettle', and the death-feeding 'crow'. The flowers are dressing her for future memory. Most suggestive

Figure 61 The ghost of Hamlet's father, from an early nineteenth-century engraving after Henry Fuseli. *A collection of prints, from pictures painted [for the Shakespeare gallery of John and Josiah Boydell], 1803. (v.2), Bodleian Library, Johnson a.59.*

of all are the 'long purples', resembling both grotesque penises and 'dead men's fingers', beckoning or snatching her towards death. And so, inevitably, she falls:

> Her clothes spread wide,
> And mermaid-like a while they bore her up;
> Which time she chanted snatches of old tunes,
> As one incapable of her own distress,
> Or like a creature native and indued
> Unto that element.
>
> (147–52)

Each moment is so lyrically visualized as to give an abiding life to the thing described. No longer quite human, Ophelia becomes a combination of spreading garment and melodious song, or a kind of water-nymph, 'a creature native and indued / Unto that element'. Her clothes take up much of the agency, liberating Ophelia 'herself' to more delicate possibilities. The garments at first resist her sinking, and in doing so create the tent from which Ophelia the water nymph can morph. Once this new form is achieved, and the songs begin to issue, the garments break off, like a cocoon, and start to cause and sustain the sinking. Once again, they take the burden, and the girl's limbs, eyes, face, even her hair, are all curiously protected, haloed by the elements. Ophelia is being reborn, or she is metamorphosing, even as she is being pulled into death. The fact that Ophelia is 'incapable of her own distress' detaches her mind (or soul) from her body. Both mind and body enter their own dimensions, each at once suffering *and* released from death. Her mind or soul is forever unclaimed by 'muddy death'; the now-spiritualized body abides in its new rebirthing element. Her 'melodious lay' is just as resistant to final death:

> But long it could not be
> Till that her garments, heavy with their drink,
> Pulled the poor wretch from her melodious lay
> To muddy death.
>
> (152–5)

Figure 62 *previous page* This famous image of *Ophelia* aestheticises her death, lifts it out of the questions of agency and will that maim the play's funeral rites, and instead places it firmly within a closely realised natural setting. John Everett Millais, Ophelia, 1862. Tate Britain/© FineArt/Alamy.

Figure 63 The head of Goliath in a Book of Hours recalls the heads of traitors that were a regular feature of London Bridge, the main route to the theatre district. Hours of Engelbert of Nassau (Flemish, 1470s), Bodleian Library, MSS. Douce 219–220, fol. 181v.

Miserere mei deus
secundum m̃
magnam miam tuã
Et secundum mul
titudinem miseratio
num tuarum dele in
iquitatem meam

ab mijn
a peccato
Quoniã
iniquita
ego cognosco
meum c
semper p
Et tibi so
malum
aut iust
monibz
aus cum
ac c

Her song does not go down to the depths. We might still hear it even as the singer has been silenced. It is no surprise that Ophelia has had so much more attention and animation in her afterlife – or more specifically in the afterlife of her dying and her death – than she ever achieved in her living actions.

The final examples of life-from-death in Shakespeare come in his late 'romances'. In these plays death happens, or is understood to have happened, despite the fact they are nominally comedies. But in each play the finality of death is redeemed, either through magical restoration or through substitutes who take up the burden of the dead life in their own.

The Tempest opens with a cataclysmic storm – 'All lost! To prayers, to prayers! All lost' (1.1.49) – but then the second scene reveals that 'there's no harm done'; it has all been the work of Prospero's art. In *Cymbeline* the doltish prince Cloten is decapitated by Guiderius, the noble prince in exile. Cloten is dead all right, but this fact barely registers. What matters is how the event contributes to the play's scheme of doubling, which pivots upon correspondences between Cloten and his rival Posthumus. They both love the heroine Innogen; both are violently lacking in faith; both indulge in pornographic fantasies of humiliation and revenge. Cloten is killed wearing Posthumus's suit; his head is tossed into the creek; Innogen thinks the headless trunk is Posthumus, and crawls upon it and weeps. The crimes of Posthumus are symbolically severed with the beheading, buried with the body, and cleansed through the mourning. Death recharges life.

In *Pericles* the queen Thaisa gives birth at sea, and the midwife enters with the baby to the anxious father:

> Take in your arms this piece
> Of your dead queen. …
> Here's all that is left living of your queen,
> A little daughter.
>
> (11.17–21)

The mother dies in childbirth; her life passes into her daughter's. This is the logic of these late comedies. A life isn't defined by a single, discrete body. It exists in relationships of surrogacy, such that one character can 'continue' the life of another. The play-world has different rules than everyday life; death can be redeemed from finality. The theme is repeated in the very next scene. Thaisa is thrown overboard in a scented coffin, which is 'belched' upon the shore by a stupendous wave and carried to the house of a magical healer, Cerimon. He opens the coffin, observes how 'fresh' the corpse looks, and by applying fire and music awakens it back into breath (12.46–95):

> Death may usurp on nature many hours,
> And yet the fire of life kindle again
>
> (12.80–81)

Perhaps she has risen from the dead; perhaps she wasn't dead at all, but merely unconscious after the trauma of birth, having 'not been entranced / Above five hours' (12.91–2). In truth it doesn't much matter which explanation we prefer. Death is a 'usurper': it is in some basic sense illegitimate. Death takes hold of things, it expresses its violence, but it isn't in this world the ultimate truth. The true thing comes into being after death, or through death – not resurrection or heaven, but the emotional longing which the savagery of death elicits. The point once again is that here is a world whose physics correspond to emotion, to desire. Death is as subject to longing, therefore, as any other active force.

It isn't that the play blithely pretends that death does not happen: quite the contrary. The daughter Marina, for instance, is to all intents an orphan. She is cast upon the charity of others and vulnerable to repeated attempts upon her life and body. She knows by heart the tale of her mother, thrown overboard, a fate which forever shadows her own ('I'll swear she's dead / And thrown into the sea', says her would-be murderer, Leonine; 15.147–8). Pericles, too, lives a life of grief and wandering, culminating in hearing of his daughter's slaughter:

> He swears
> Never to wash his face, nor cut his hairs.
> He puts on sack-cloth, and to sea. He bears
> A tempest which his mortal vessel tears,
> And yet he rides it out.
>
> (18.27–31)

He enters a living death, lost from community, an embodiment of mourning, his 'mortal vessel' torn by the storm – and yet surviving. Pericles suffers the other side of a world where death is not the end. And it isn't the end because all we can *know* of death is that it kills over and over those who survive it. He has no choice but to 'ride it out'.

The play's wishful, romantic ending observes the same rules. The child returns from death to the father, the wife to the husband, the mother to the daughter. But in all of these returns it remains *death* that is finding expression. Death generates the longing for life. This is our only experience of death, and plays can make it come true.

The same basic pattern is found in *The Winter's Tale*. On the one hand, deaths that return to or give way to life; on the other, a persisting recognition that while death is inevitable, we survive in its wake. Art is made in the face of death, as rival, compensation or denial. The 'good' young Sicilian prince Mamillius dies upon hearing of his mother's dishonour; his death kills the mother, Hermione; her ghost appears to Antigonus, who must deliver her newborn 'bastard' to the wild coast of Bohemia; this marks the end of Antigonus, eaten by a bear, and the end too of the sailors (presumably his Sicilian countrymen), whose ship goes down in the accompanying storm. But then the shepherds who witness the eaten gentleman and the drowning sailors come upon the swaddled child: 'things dying' give way to 'things new-born' (3.3.111). Romance logic takes over.

The scene leaps sixteen years, and there is a new young prince courting the beautiful shepherdess: together they repair the loss of Mamillius. The lovers return

Figure 64 Pericles leads a life of grief and wandering, haunted by the near-death experience of the opening scenes. His reunion with his wife and daughter exemplifies the return from the dead that is such a feature of Shakespeare's later plays. The quarto edition of 1609 is shown here, together with the title page of the 1619 quarto, now bound into one volume. Bodleian Library, Arch. G d.41 (5).

Per. Heauens make a Starre of him, yet there my
Queene, wee'le celebrate their Nuptialls, and our selues
will in that kingdome spend our following daies, our sonne
and daughter shall in *Tyrus* raigne.
 Lord *Cerimon* wee doe our longing stay,
To heare the rest vntolde, Sir lead's the way.

FINIS.

Gower.

In *Antiochus* and his daughter you haue heard
Of monstrous lust, the due and iust reward:
In *Pericles* his Queene and Daughter seene,
Although assayl'de with *Fortune* fierce and keene.
 Vertue preferd from fell destructions blast,
 Lead on by heauen, and crown'd with ioy at last.
In *Helycanus* may you well descrie,
A figure of trueth, of faith, of loyaltie:
In reuerend *Cerimon* there well appeares,
The worth that learned charitie aye weares,
 For wicked *Cleon* and his wife, when Fame
 Had spred his cursed deede, the honor'd name
Of *Pericles*, to rage the Cittie turne,
That him and his they in his Pallace burne:
The gods for murder seemde so content,
To punish, although not done, but meant.
 So on your Patience euermore attending,
 New ioy wayte on you, heere our play has ending.

FINIS.

THE LATE,
And much admired Play,
CALLED,
Pericles, Prince of Tyre.

With the true Relation of the whole Hi-
story, aduentures, and fortunes of
the saide Prince.

Written by W. Shakespeare.

Printed for T. P. 1619.

to Sicily, where the guilty king has grieved daily for the wife and heir he had effectively killed. A statue is unveiled of his dead wife – and the statue moves, and then speaks:

But how, is to be questioned, for I saw her,
As I thought, dead; and have in vain said many
A prayer upon her grave.

(5.3.140–42)

There are no absolute answers to the mystery. Was she hidden away for sixteen years, as her companion Paulina claims? Has the statue been animated, à la Pygmalion? Has the dead Hermione come to life? Logistical or miraculous explanations hang unresolved in the air, allowing for the more primary fact that the grief and longing generated by death are *answered*. Answered, but in such a way as to confirm rather than erase their reality. Grief and longing are so fierce and durable as to always warrant stories like this, in which the lost souls return from death. This is why the closing happiness of the 'precious winners all' is balanced by Paulina's undying memory of one particular death:

I, an old turtle,
Will wing me to some withered bough, and there
My mate, that's never to be found again,
Lament, till I am lost.

(5.3.133–6)

Figure 65 A Book of Hours illustrating the Last Judgement: the souls exist in monochrome against the colours of heavenly salvation. It's striking that so few of Shakespeare's dying characters are concerned with this Christian paradigm. Hours of Engelbert of Nassau (Flemish, 1470s), Bodleian Library, MSS. Douce 219–220, fol. 190v.

Shakespeare leaves the balance hanging. Sad or happy, it is death that gives the point to all that is 'Performed in this wide gap of time' – a gap, as these plays always know, between two abysses.

Mr Ben: Johnson and Mr Wm Shakespear
Being Merrye att a Tauern, Mr Jonson hauing
begune this for his Epitaph

87   Here lies Ben Johnson that was once one
he giues yt Wm Shakspear to make vpp who pfeatly writts
who while hee liude was a sloe thinge
And now being dead is Nothinge
                    finis

4   341   On Sr Maryotte att westminster vppon
                    on John Flower

88   Here lies John Flower vnder this stone
who serued god while hee was here, and now to him is gone
A Gentleman, and A Head Borrough a good man In his House
who Maried was to diuers wiues, & was to euch of them a kind spouse
Hee left the world departed hence the 23 of may
In the yeare of o lo: god 1567 being whitson mondaye
                    finis

342ª   On Mr Georg Heyward father to Sr
        Rowland Heyward, lo: Maior of London

89   Interred here George Heyward is and Margarett his wyfe
God blessed them wth Children six, yay led a vertuous life
Sonns to, and Daughters fower, by name Gilbert & Sr Rowland
A knight his Mother happie birth, yt firstly all weare found
Alice, Katharine, Elianor, and Ann; In June here did
the yeares of Christ the figurs shew 1597 In tyme what will not slide
Allthough, hee was full 4 score yeares & I, his wife also
In the yeare of o lord 1597 of hir owne age 97 from ys to god did goe
                    finis

342ᵇ   vppon Judge Owen and Judge Richardson
        both buried In westminster neare on
        a nother

90   Here lies Judge Owen that neuer tooke bribes
    Here lies Judge Richardson, that neuer denied
                    finis; Jgnoto

        343   On Sr Robert Dudley Earle of warwicke
            and Leicster

91

Coda: *Afterlives*

Shakespeare's death in 1616 received little public comment: perhaps, withdrawn from the London theatre world in Stratford, he was out of mind. The comparison with the outpouring at the death of his theatrical collaborator in the King's Men, the first Othello, Hamlet, Richard III and Lear, Richard Burbage, some three years later, is striking. Middleton called it an 'eclipse of playing', the third Earl of Pembroke excused himself from attending a play as he mourned 'the loss of my old acquaintance Burbadg', and one anonymous wit used the succinct form of a stage direction: '_____ Exit Burbage', its long dash imitating the form in which an exit cue was written on an actor's part. Now, wrote another elegist, poets should give up writing tragedies because 'since tragic parts you see / die all with him'.[30] The actor, like the monarch in the influential medieval theory, has two bodies: his body dramatic – or his characters – and his body physical. Having performed the death of the body dramatic hundreds of times, only now, with his physical death, are Hamlet, Othello and Lear really dead. Burbage's death was understood as resolving that deeply Shakespearean paradox – those lively, feigned or ambiguous deaths in his plays.

Shakespeare's own death, however, received less attention. A single manuscript elegy, by William Basse, called him a 'rare tragedian'. His monument in Holy Trinity Church, Stratford-upon-Avon, made no mention of his literary career,

Figure 66 This commonplace book of the early seventeenth century reports an anecdote of Shakespeare and Jonson in a tavern together writing their own epitaphs. Scarcely any epitaphs for the death of Shakespeare in 1616 are known. Bodleian Library, MS. Ashmole 38, p. 181.

and the lines on his tomb have been felt by many to be embarrassing doggerel unworthy of the poet:

Good friend for Jesus' sake forebear,
To dig the dust enclosed here.
Blest be the man that spares these stones,
And curst be he that moves my bones.

There have been a number of proposed schemes to defy or circumvent this curse. In 1856 Delia Bacon, in search of evidence that her namesake Francis Bacon had actually written the plays, spent the night in the church in Stratford but seems to have lost her nerve about excavating Shakespeare's grave. Mark Twain's squib 'Is Shakespeare Dead?' explores the Bacon authorship theory. Stories circulated throughout the nineteenth century that the vault had indeed been opened.[31] In 1883 C.M Ingleby published *Shakespeare's Bones: The Proposal to Disinter Them, Considered in Relation to Their Possible Bearing on His Portraiture*. George Bernard Shaw's oft-quoted dislike of Shakespeare – 'it would positively be a relief to me to dig him up and throw stones at him' – needs to be seen in this pervasive exhumatory context. As recently as 2015 a South African academic renewed his call for Shakespeare's remains to be dug up to discover more about the cause of his death. In the early twentieth century, communicating with Shakespeare through spiritualism was surprisingly common: the important editor of the Variorum edition, H.H. Furness, and the Shakespearean critic G. Wilson Knight were both spiritualists. Communing beyond the grave with Shakespeare to discover his secrets has been a perennial fantasy: when the ghost of Shakespeare did stalk the stage in the epilogue to Charles Gildon's Restoration rewriting of *Measure for Measure* (1700) he complained bitterly: 'Enough your cruelty alive I knew, / And Must I dead by persecuted too? / Injured so much of late upon the Stage, / My ghost can bear no more.'[32]

As this ghost acknowledges, if Shakespeare's mortal remains have been – largely – undisturbed in Stratford since 1616, the same cannot be said for those

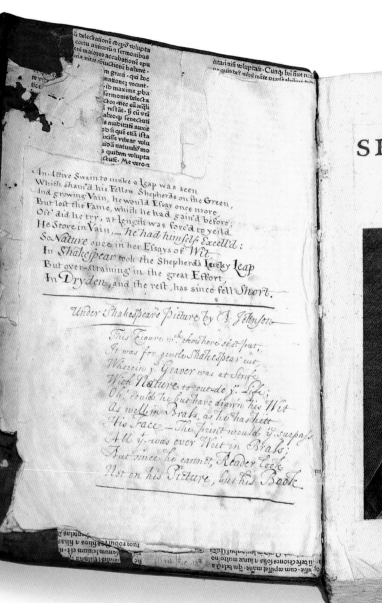

An Active Swain to make a Leap was seen,
Which sham'd his Fellow Shepherds on the Green;
And growing Vain, he would Essay once more,
But lost the Fame, which he had gain'd before;
Oft' did he try, at length was forc'd to yeild
He Strove in Vain, — he had himself Excell'd:
So Nature once in her Essays of Wit
In Shakespear took the Shepherd's Lucky Leap
But over-straining in the great Effort,
In Dryden, and the rest, has since fell Short.

Under Shakespear's Picture by B. Johnson

This Figure w.ch thou here see'st put,
It was for gentle Shakespear cut,
Wherein y.e Graver was at Strife
With Nature to out-do y.e Life;
Oh, could he but have drawn his Wit
As well in Brass, as he has hitt
His Face — The Print would y.n surpass,
All y.t was ever Writ in Brass;
But since he cannot, Reader look
Not on his Picture, but his Book

Mr. WILLIAM
SHAKESPEARES
COMEDIES,
HISTORIES, &
TRAGEDIES.

Published according to the True Originall Copies.

works that would keep him forever alive. 'Thou art a monument without a tomb', wrote Ben Jonson in a prefatory poem to the First Folio of 1623, 'And art alive still while thy book doth live'. Other poets echoed the conceit in this first posthumous collection of Shakespeare's plays: 'for though his line of life went soon about / The life yet of his lines shall never out' and 'our Shakespeare, thou canst never die, / But crowned with laurel, live eternally.' His fellow actors John Heminge and Henry Condell boasted that the Folio collection was, as in a kind of textual Last Judgement, a resurrection and perfection of a scattered and broken body: 'as where, before, you were abused with divers stolen and surreptitious copies, maimed and deformed by the frauds and stealths of injurious imposters that exposed them, even those are now offered to your view cured and perfect of their limbs'. The rhetoric of the Folio edition is monumental, memorial. And it is true that without this book, which gathered up previously unpublished playscripts and preserved them in a robust folio format, much of Shakespeare would have been lost, and the history of his reputation over four centuries would have looked very different (Figure 67).

'Shakespeare's dead' is thus only narrowly true. Just as many of Shakespeare's dead (characters) turn out not to be, so too the death of their author may be another fiction. A glance at contemporary culture, at theatre, at the English language, at YouTube, at political rhetoric, at literature, would suggest that his death, like that of his Innogen or Hero, is a fiction. Like Falstaff he 'riseth up'; like Hamlet's father he returns from beyond the grave; like Hermione he steps down from his pedestal. New fictions resume the undead lives of Ophelia or Macbeth, or recover *The Tempest*'s Ariel from where Shakespeare left him, beneath the blossom under the bough, and make him the avatar of some new post-human dispensation. A recent graphic novel series, *Kill Shakespeare*, sets the heroes of the plays against the villains in a quest to seize the author's quill and with it the power to change reality. At the time of writing, the sequence is unfinished. Its very existence is the antidote to its teleological premiss. So long as people are writing comic books – or quoting, adapting, analysing, performing, translating or exhibiting Shakespeare – rumours of his death seem to be greatly exaggerated.

Figure 68 The attribution of this poem, 'Shall I dye', to Shakespeare in the 1630s has been controversial and most scholars are deeply unconvinced. But if it is not by Shakespeare, this addition to his canon gives us a glimpse of his posthumous reputation in the process of being corroborated. Bodleian Library, MS. Rawl. poet. 160, fols. 107v–108r.

A SONNET

1

It is not long since I could see
And when the day did rise
I knew twas light, but now from me
Tis hidden in yo.r eyes

2

Then, sweetest, since I only know
to Judge by your bright way
Shine to your selfe for I will goe
I sweare none other way

3

There I may see in yo.r sweet frame
heavens mold with all its bliss
Which though not mortall eie could name
Ile taste it in a kisse

4

Yet by not voice can I.ere find
my sight if you not showe
Vp on faire beames, Ile still be blind
Ruled Ime turn'd by you,

A SONNET

1

Thou sentst to me a heart was sound,
I tooke it to be thine
But when I saw it had a wound,
I knew ye heart was myne

2

A conceite of a strong conceipt
to send myne owne to me
And send it in a worse estate
Then when it came to thee

3

The heart I sent thee had noe staine
It was intire and sound,
But thou hast sent it backe againe
Sick of a deadly wound

4

O hard! how wouldst thou vse a heart
that should rebellious be
Since thou hast slayne myne w.th a dart
that soe much honor'd thee.
finis

1

Shall I dye, shall I flye
loveus baits, and deceipts
sorrow breeding
Shall I tend shall I send
shall I shewe, and not rue
my proceeding
In all duty, her beawty
Binds me her servant, for ever
If she scorne, I mourne
I retire, to despaire
Joying never.

2

Yet I must, vent my lust
and explaine, inward paine
by my soul breeding
If she smiled, etc eyled
all my moane, if she frownd
all my hoped deceaving
Suspitious doubt, oh keepe out
For thou art my tormentor
Fly away, parke away
I will loue for loue
bid me venter

3

T'were abuse to accuse
my faire loue, er I proue
her affection
therefore try her reply
greed thee Joy, or annoy
or affliction
yet how ere I will beard
Her pleasure with patience for beawty,
sure will not seeme to blot
Her deserts wronging him,
doth her duty.

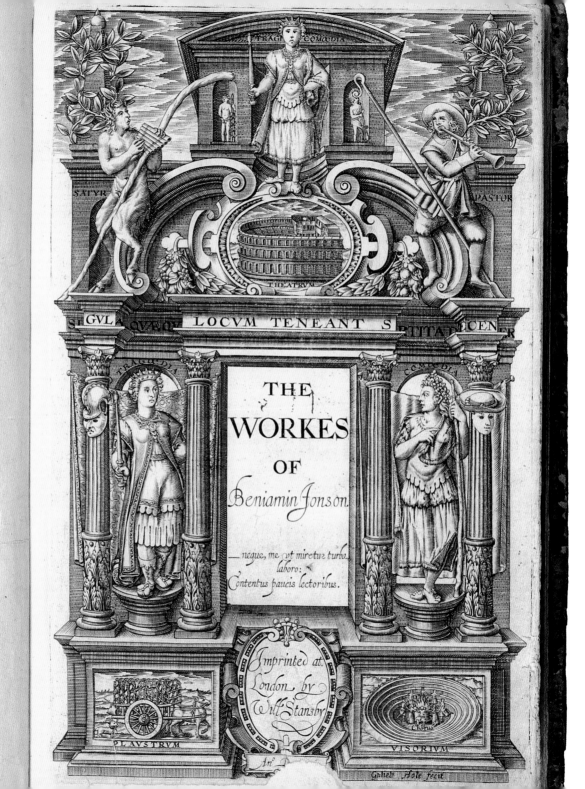

Notes

1. Robert N. Watson, *The Rest is Silence: Death as Annihilation in the English Renaissance* (Berkeley and London: University of California Press, 1994), p. 7.

2. Arthur Miller, *Collected Plays* (London: Cresset, 1958), p.33.

3. Stephen Greenblatt, *Hamlet in Purgatory* (Princeton NJ and Oxford: Princeton University Press, 2001), p. 240.

4. Thomas Lupset, *A compendious and a very fruteful treatyse, teachynge the waye of dyenge well* (London, 1534), pp. 92, 103–4.

5. Watson, *The Rest is Silence*, p. 3.

6. John Fletcher, *The Faithful Shepherdess* (London, 1609).

7. Thomas Lodge, *A Treatise of the Plague* (London, 1603), sig. C3.

8. Ernest B. Gilman, *Plague Writing in Early Modern England* (Chicago: University of Chicago Press, 2009) p. 35.

9. Thomas Dekker, *The Wonderful Year* (London, 1603), sig. E2v.

10. Quoted in Tanya Pollard, *Shakespeare's Theater: A Sourcebook* (Malden MA and Oxford: Blackwell, 2004), p. 322.

11. Steven Mullaney, *The Place of the Stage: License, Play and Power in Renaissance England* (Chicago: University of Chicago Press, 1988), p. 50.

12. William Prynne, *Histrio-Mastix: The Players Scourge, or, Actors Tragaedie* (1632), quoted in Darryl Chalk. "'A nature but infected': Plague and Embodied Transformation in *Timon of Athens*', *Early Modern Literary Studies*, Special Issue 19(9) (2009), pp. 1–28, http://purl.oclc.org/emls/si-19/chalplag.html.

13. Dekker, *The Wonderful Year*, sig.D.

14. Ibid., sig C4v.

15. René Girard, 'The Plague in Literature and Myth', *Texas Studies in Literature and Language* 15 (1974), pp. 833–50; 834.

16. Thomas Dekker, *News from Gravesend* (London, 1604), sigs E2–E3.

17. Dekker, *Wonderful Year*, sig. C4v.

18. Watson, *The Rest is Silence*, p. 98.

19. Michael Neill, *Issues of Death: Mortality and Identity in English Renaissance Drama* (Oxford: Clarendon Press, 1997), p. 1.

20. Sigmund Freud, 'Beyond the Pleasure Principle', in *The Complete Psychological Works of Sigmund Freud*, vol. 18 (London: Vintage Classics, 2001), p. 44.

21. J.B. Steane (ed.), *The Unfortunate Traveller and Other Works* (Harmondsworth: Penguin, 1972), p. 113.

22. Greenblatt, *Hamlet in Purgatory*, p. 258.

23. Marvin Carlson, *The Haunted Stage: The Theatre as Memory Machine* (Ann Arbor: University of Michigan Press, 2001).

24. R.B. Outhwaite (1985), quoted in Emma Smith (ed.), *Shakespeare in Production: King Henry V* (Cambridge: Cambridge University Press, 2002), p. 8.

25. William Camden, *Britain: A Chorographical Description* (London, 1637), p. 118.

26. Curtis C. Breight, *Surveillance, Militarism and Drama in the Elizabethan Era* (London: Macmillan, 1996), p. 232.

27. See Smith (ed.), *Shakespeare in Production: King Henry V*, p. 49.

28. *In Parenthesis*, quoted in ibid., p. 44.

29. Henry Jackson, 'Letter to "G.P."', Sep. 1610, Corpus Christi *Fulman* papers, X. 83r–84v; translation from Gamini Salgado (ed.), *Eyewitnesses of Shakespeare* (New York: Barnes & Noble, 1975), p. 30.

30. Bart van Es, *Shakespeare in Company* (Oxford: Oxford University Press, 2013), p. 234.

31. Samuel Schoenbaum, *Shakespeare's Lives* (Oxford: Clarendon Press, 1970), pp. 471–3.

32. Charles Gildon, *Beauty, the Best Advocate* (London, 1700), n.pag.

Figure 69 Ben Jonson's 1616 Folio collection of his works was the model for the 1623 volume of Shakespeare's works selected by Heminge and Condell. Bodleian Library, Arch. A d.28.

Further Reading

Marvin Carlson, *The Haunted Stage: The Theatre as Memory Machine* (Ann Arbor: University of Michigan Press, 2001).

Sigmund Freud, 'Beyond the Pleasure Principle', in *The Complete Psychological Works of Sigmund Freud*, vol. 18 (London: Vintage Classics, 2001).

Ernest B. Gilman, *Plague Writing in Early Modern England* (Chicago: University of Chicago Press, 2009).

René Girard, 'The Plague in Literature and Myth', *Texas Studies in Literature and Language* 15 (1974).

Stephen Greenblatt, *Hamlet in Purgatory* (Princeton NJ and Oxford: Princeton University Press, 2001).

Thomas Lupset, *A compendious and a very fruteful treatyse, teachynge the waye of dyenge well* (London, 1534).

Arthur Miller, *Collected Plays* (London: Cresset, 1958).

Steven Mullaney, *The Place of the Stage: License, Play and Power in Renaissance England* (Chicago: University of Chicago Press, 1988).

Michael Neill, *Issues of Death: Mortality and Identity in English Renaissance Drama* (Oxford: Clarendon Press, 1997).

Simon Palfrey, *Shakespeare's Possible Worlds* (Cambridge: Cambridge University Press, 2014).

Simon Palfrey, *Poor Tom: Living 'King Lear'* (Chicago: University of Chicago Press, 2015).

Tanya Pollard, *Shakespeare's Theater: A Sourcebook* (Oxford and Malden MA: Blackwell, 2004).

Samuel Schoenbaum, *Shakespeare's Lives* (Oxford: Clarendon Press, 1970).

Emma Smith (ed.), *Shakespeare in Production: King Henry V* (Cambridge: Cambridge University Press, 2002).

J.B. Steane (ed.), *The Unfortunate Traveller and Other Works* (Harmondsworth: Penguin, 1972).

Geoffrey Tillotson, 'Othello and *The Alchemist* at Oxford', *Times Literary Suplement*, 20 July 1933, p. 494.

Bart van Es, *Shakespeare in Company* (Oxford: Oxford University Press, 2013).

Robert N. Watson, *The Rest is Silence: Death as Annihilation in the English Renaissance* (Berkeley and London: University of California Press, 1994).

F.P. Wilson, *The Plague Pamphlets of Thomas Dekker* (Oxford: Clarendon Press, 1925).

Figure 70 Illustration from the late-sixteenth-century album of Jan van der Deck. Bodleian Library, MS. Rawl. B. 21, fol. 42r.

Index

References to illustrations are in italics